The Search Press Book of
Traditional Papercrafts

For papercrafters around the world,
past present and future.

The Search Press Book of
TRADITIONAL PAPERCRAFTS

Parchment Craft, Stencil Embossing, Paper Pricking, Quilling

JANET WILSON

SEARCH PRESS

Contents

THE ART OF
Paper Pricking

THE ART OF
Quilling

Introduction

My interest in paper started in early childhood, when I was given some paper and a pair of scissors. Since then, I have also developed interests in medieval history, ancient civilisations, religions, and mythology. This mixture perhaps explains my passion for traditional papercrafts.

Many ancient and traditional crafts are being cast aside in the race to modernise cultures throughout the world. How sad it would be if we lost such a rich heritage of crafts, most of which have been lovingly passed down from person to person over the ages. For some of the papercrafts there were no written instructions available at the time of my research and no clue as to their origin.

Research of traditional crafts takes time and determination – you have to delve into their historical backgrounds and development through the centuries, and this can take several years before the whole 'picture' is revealed. My research for this book has enabled me to sympathetically update the traditional techniques and I have been able to keep the soul of these papercrafts intact as far as possible when designing the patterns and projects.

It has given me the chance to put instructions and patterns into print, and to ensure that future generations, who may be as intrigued as I am about papercrafts, have access to that information. Thus these ancient and traditional arts will never be lost.

The book contains four of the many old papercrafts that have interested me. You do not need to be an artist to be able to do any of them, and modern tools and materials have made all these crafts much easier. I hope they intrigue you and give you as many happy hours of creativity as they have done me.

The Art of
Parchment Craft

The origins of this beautiful and ancient art are
somewhat obscure, but it is believed to have
developed from bookbinding as practised in
Spain before Columbus discovered the New
World. Examples of such bookbinding can be
seen in the British Library. The parchment was
dipped in a medium that made it translucent,
then embossing and piercing was skilfully
applied to decorate it.

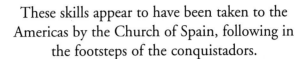

These skills appear to have been taken to the Americas by the Church of Spain, following in the footsteps of the conquistadors.

The craft has since evolved to card- and box-making with translucent paper. Although the basic principles of parchment craft – embossing, perforating and cutting – are the same all over the world, artists in Mexico, Brazil, Peru and Colombia all have distinct types of work.

No colour was used in the original craft except, perhaps, a little gold embellishment. Colouring the work is a twentieth-century addition and today's parchment crafters are divided into those who prefer the original white work and those who like the addition of colour.

In this section I show you the basic techniques of white work, then how to use various forms of colour. Simple projects show you how to make gift cards, bookmarks, picture frames and even three-dimensional objects.

Materials

Parchment craft materials can be found in art and craft shops or via mail order specialists. Specially made paper-embossing and needle tools are used to create the beautiful patterns and lace-like designs shown throughout this book.

Parchment paper

This is a type of transcript paper (3). The weight most widely used is 140/150g. The paper should be fairly supple; some papers are brittle and they crack very easily when embossed, so try out a small piece first before investing in a large quantity.

Tracing

Pens (5)   You will need a mapping pen for non-metallic inks and I would recommend that you use a steel-nibbed pen for the metallic inks.

White pencil (6)   Use a white pencil to trace fine lines that require embossing. Embossing over white ink will make the traced line go black.

Embossing

Pads (4)   You can buy special embossing pads in different sizes. However, you can also use something like a padded diary – the sort with a plastic covering over a thin sponge insert.

Tools (7)   The working ends of these tools are small ball-shaped points of different sizes. In general, the smaller points produce the most intense white images (see page 13 for details of sizes used in this book). Similar tools are used for paper embossing.

Perforating

Pads (13)   Again you can buy perforating pads designed for this craft but you can use a piece of thick felt or a thick mouse mat, sponge side up. For multiple needle tools such as the 7-needle and half-circle tool, a thin rubber mat on a piece of cardboard works well.

Needle tools (12)   There are lots of different needle tools available. The patterns in this book are designed for tools with needles set 1mm apart. In certain parts of the world you can buy tools with thicker needles that are set slightly wider apart. If you use these larger tools, especially the 4-needle tool for lace borders, amend the designs to allow for the wider pitch. All the tools used in this book are illustrated on page 13.

Scissors (9)   Use curved cuticle scissors with very fine tips for cutting lace grids to crosses and slots. A pair of deckle-edged or pinking scissors can be used to trim the edges of some cards.

Colouring

Inks (1)   Use any waterproof or acrylic inks.

Paints (2)   Most types of acrylic paints work well.

Oil pastels (15)   There are a number of brands available on the market. You need to use ones that do not 'crumb'. Use odourless barbecue igniter or white spirit as a spreading medium.

Watercolour pencils (11)   There are a number of brands on the market and most work well.

Felt-tip pens (10)   Any water-soluble felt-tip pens can be used to good effect.

Brushes (8)   You will need a No. 2 round brush for general work. You will also find a spotter and a No. 4 shader brush useful.

Other materials

You will also need a ruler (14), some kitchen paper, a pair of sharp-ended tweezers, a water pot, narrow double-sided sticky tape, clear silicone glue and some wooden cocktail sticks, a bunch of stamens with tiny heads, a few tiny pearl beads . . . and a lot of patience.

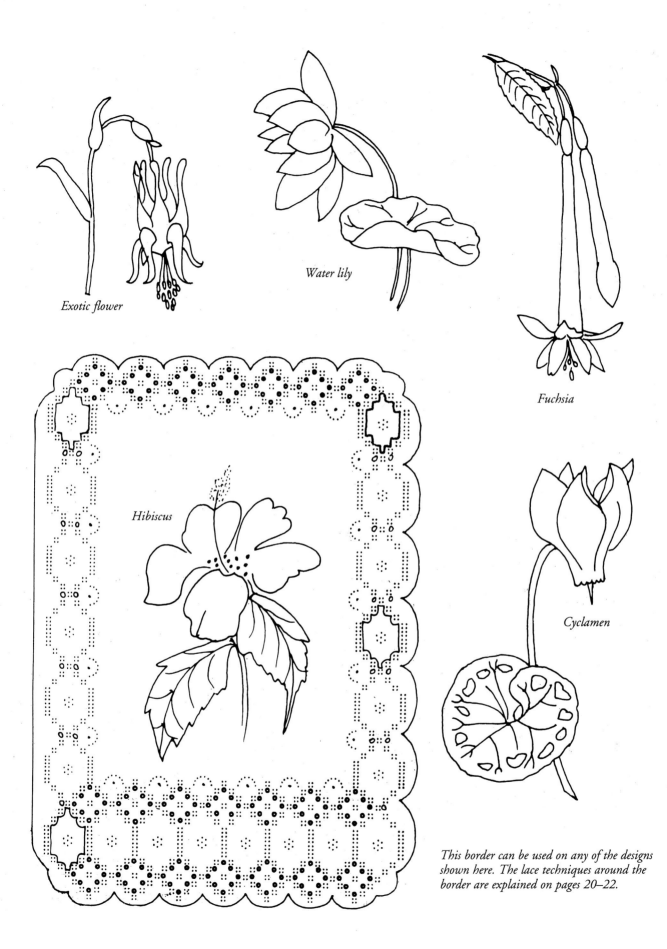

Exotic flower

Water lily

Fuchsia

Hibiscus

Cyclamen

This border can be used on any of the designs shown here. The lace techniques around the border are explained on pages 20–22.

White work

Before you start adding colour, you must first learn the techniques of tracing the design, embossing it and then perforating a lace border. In this section, I have included a practice sheet containing various designs that look good as white images. The practice sheet also includes a border that you can perforate and use to surround all of the designs. For the tracing and embossing exercises I have used the water lily design, and for the perforating exercise, I have used the fuchsia design.

Tools

The exercises in this chapter require the following tools:

Tracing   For white work trace the design with a mapping pen and white acrylic ink. Other colours, especially sepia and antelope brown, are used for coloured images. A sharp white pencil is useful for tracing continuous fine lines in borders – and it can be erased if you make a mistake.

Embossing   Use a combination of three tools to build up effects: the 4mm plastic-headed tool to warm up the paper and produce soft white effects; then the 3, 1.5 and 1mm steel tools (depending on the effect you want to achieve) to complete the image; and a stylus, which has a sharp point, for embossing very fine lines in borders. You can also use the 3 and 4mm tools to smooth out any lumpy embossing made with the finer tools.

Stippling   I have included a needle tool which, although not essential, I find useful for creating fine texture.

Perforating   For the border given on the practice sheet you need the 1-, 2-, 4- and 7-needle tools and the half-circle needle tool. Use your scissors to cut to crosses and slots. I also illustrate a 3-needle tool used in some of the other borders in this section.

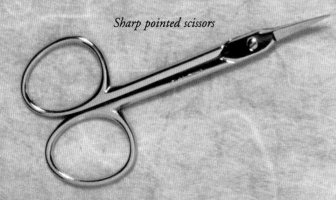

Sharp pointed scissors

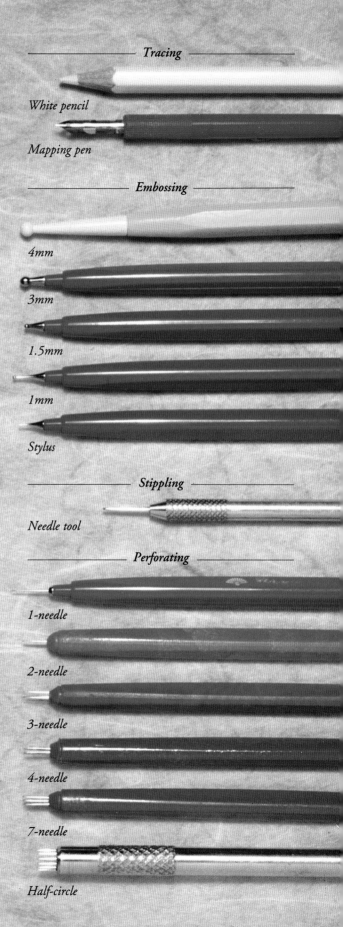

Tracing

White pencil

Mapping pen

Embossing

4mm

3mm

1.5mm

1mm

Stylus

Stippling

Needle tool

Perforating

1-needle

2-needle

3-needle

4-needle

7-needle

Half-circle

Tracing

This simple technique is one of the most important features of parchment craft; you need to have an outlined shape within which to work.

Practise the tracing techniques before you begin, so that you do not spoil your first design. If you have a wobbly hand, it may help to rest it on the embossing pad while tracing.

The traced line must be as fine as possible, and this is governed by the way you hold the pen, not the size of the nib. Dipping a new nib in boiling water will improve its writing qualities. Wipe it dry with kitchen paper before dipping it into the ink.

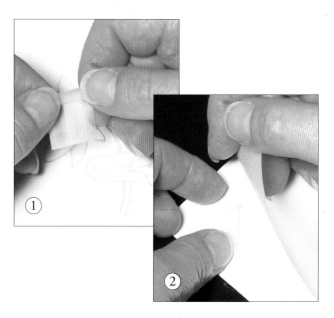

1. Carefully position the parchment paper over the pattern. Roll two small pieces of tape into cylinders, with the sticky sides outermost.

2. Lift the top corner of the parchment paper and, avoiding the design area, place a sticky roll between the pattern and the parchment paper. Press lightly to secure the paper so that it does not slip when you are tracing.

3. Shake the ink well, then fill the nib using the dropper. If you do not have a dropper, simply dip the pen into the ink.

4. Start to trace the design. Hold the pen upright and let it skate across the surface very lightly to get a fine line. The more pressure you apply on the nib, the thicker the line will be.

TIP: Keeping your nib clean

- When the nib reservoir empties, wipe the nib on a small sponge soaked in water before dipping it in the ink again. When you have finished tracing, clean the nib and dry it with kitchen paper before putting the pen away.

TIP: Tracing fine lines in borders

- Embossing over an ink-traced line will make the ink go black, and it is also virtually impossible to follow a fine line with an embossing tool. By using a white pencil, you can erase any mistakes with a rubber.

Embossing

Embossing is achieved by rubbing the rounded point of an embossing tool over the surface of a sheet of parchment paper laid on the soft side of an embossing pad. Rubbing causes the fibres of the paper to be displaced and bruised which results in a change of colour – it also makes the paper more elastic, allowing you to increase the pressure and, subsequently, to whiten the colour further.

The more you rub the paper surface, the whiter the result will be. Work from side to side within a traced area; do not go round and round to start with, or you will get a small black mark in the middle of your working area.

Use a selection of tools as an artist uses his colour palette – but instead of painting in colour, use the tools to produce shades of white. In general, the larger the embossing tip, the greyer the effect, and the smaller it is, the whiter the effect.

You can emboss on both side of the paper to produce concave and convex shapes; this will help create depth in your images.

It is important to make sure that you have a balanced visual effect, i.e. not too much white or grey in any one area. The focal point of your finished piece will be the whitest area, so bear this in mind before you begin.

1. Trace the water lily design. Look at the design and decide which parts need concave embossing, and which need convex embossing. For those of you unfamiliar with these terms, look at the two pictures of my hand which show the shapes. Mark the design to show the shapes as shown above – the letter 'A' represents the concave shapes which are embossed from the front, and the letter 'B' the convex ones which are embossed from the back.

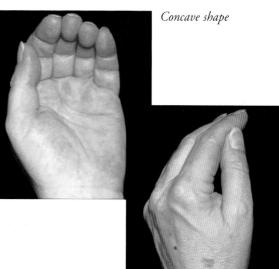

Concave shape

Convex shape

TIP: Embossing

- When embossing remember the shape of the petals. I have seen some flowers that look like flying saucers because they have been embossed too hard from edge to edge.
- Petal edges should sink back into the paper. Emboss the central area of the petal and then soften the embossing as you reach the edges.

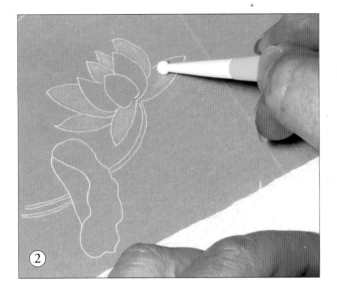

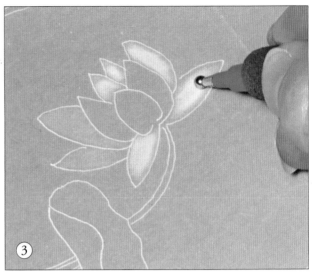

2. Place the parchment paper (with the tracing uppermost) on the soft side of your embossing pad, and a piece of plain paper on which to rest your hands, just below the design. Start embossing with the 4mm plastic tool; its large ball tip is excellent for undercoating and produces a good base grey tone. Rub the area within each petal outline (shape A), working gently from side to side. Exert more pressure each time you rub, until the paper starts to discolour.

3. When all the concave petals have been undercoated, change to the 3mm steel tool and start to whiten the central areas of each petal. Work over the undercoat, carefully embossing selected areas to give shape and form. Do not work over the traced lines with a steel tool, as this will turn them black. Work down the design, keeping the paper firmly in position as you build up the embossing.

TIP: Waxing the embossing tools

Keep a small pot of wax on the work surface when you are embossing your designs and use this to lubricate the tools frequently to keep them smooth. This will lessen any friction between the ball tips and the paper surface when you are rubbing the areas to be embossed.

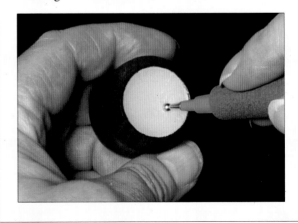

4. Go back to the 4mm tool and emboss out to the edges of the petals; try to emphasize the curve of each petal by graduating the tones of white.

5. Now change to the stylus and, with its sharp point, accentuate the tips of the petals. Use the stylus like the other embossing tools, working from side to side or up and down to build up white highlights.

6. When you have finished all the concave-shaped petals, turn the parchment paper over and work the convex petals as described in stages 2–5.

7. Without turning the paper over, use the 1.5mm tool to create a lip round the edges of some of the concave petals (shape A). Gradually increase the pressure until the desired effect is achieved.

8. Shape and form can be worked into a chosen area. Here, the main petal is an important part of the design, and to give it form, turn the paper over and emboss a loop shape around the petal edge using the 3mm tool.

The finished design, without a border. Check the front of the design frequently when you are using the different tools, to check your progress as you go along. If the petals look grey, rubbing them harder should produce a white, raised design. Keep working on the shape, form and colour until you are happy with the result.

Stippling fine detail

For the fine markings of the anthers on the long stamen in the hibiscus design, use a stippling tool or a 1-needle tool to create a stippled effect. Place the design on a piece of strong card and move the tool up and down with small rapid movements, puncturing the paper with a series of small dots. This is a useful technique that can be used for the centres of lots of other flowers.

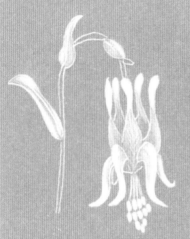

Water Lily. *The leaf turnover was worked with C-shaped strokes of the embossing tool, working from the fold line up to the top, to give an impression of depth.*

Exotic flower. *Make the petal tips white and shade the other parts to create shape. Use the stylus or a needle to draw in the central and side veins on the front upright petal.*

Fuchsia. *Decide on which side of the flower head the light is coming from and then emboss the long tube with the heaviest strokes on the light side.*

Cyclamen. *The right-hand petal is embossed on both sides of the paper. The turnover part, nearest the central petal, is embossed from the back, while the remainder of it is embossed from the front to give form to the petal.*

Hibiscus. *With this flower it is most important to use curved strokes of the embossing tool to make each petal appear more lifelike.*

Perforating

When you are happy with your tracing and embossing skills try using the perforating technique to create a border round the design. Lace grid patterns are the foundation of delicate lace-like borders. Here I use the fuchsia design to fill the central space but any of the designs given on the practice sheet will fit.

> **TIP: Using lace grid patterns**
>
> Lace grid patterns can only be used twice before they are destroyed by the perforations, so I suggest photocopying them before you start.

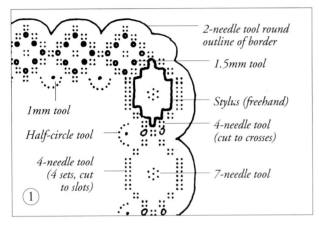

2-needle tool round outline of border
1.5mm tool
Stylus (freehand)
4-needle tool (cut to crosses)
7-needle tool
1mm tool
Half-circle tool
4-needle tool (4 sets, cut to slots)

1. Look at the design and decide on the tools you need. I have annotated a detail of the border pattern used in this exercise to show those needed here.

2. Secure the parchment over the pattern (see page 14) and then use a white pencil to trace the scalloped border.

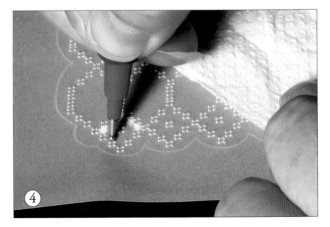

3. Using the 4-needle tool, mark the four-point lace grid. Marking is a partial perforation – the needles should only just break through the paper. Trace the fuchsia design in the middle with a mapping pen and white ink.

4. Remove the paper from the pattern, turn it over and place it on your embossing pad. Emboss the fuchsia and then the sets of eight small circles in the border design with the 1.5mm tool.

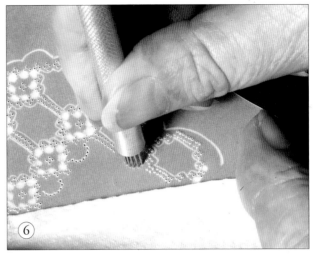

5. Following the traced white pencil line, emboss the scalloped, outside edge of the border with the stylus. Next, use the same tool freehand to draw in the small panels within the lace pattern. The sharp point of the stylus will give a fine white line, creating a delicate embossed effect on the finished design.

6. Still working on the back of the parchment paper, use the half-circle needle tool to complete the inside edges of the border. Working from the back adds texture to the front of the design.

7. Change to the 7-needle tool and perforate the circles in the centre of each small panel, again working from the back to the front.

8. Reperforate the whole lace grid border with the 4-needle tool to make the holes bigger. Turn the paper over and re-perforate the half-circle and 7-needle tool work as well.

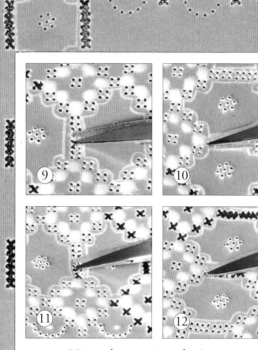

9–12. Using sharp, pointed scissors, cut the 4-needle grid to slots. Insert the tips of the scissors between the first two holes in the long side of a slot area and snip the gap. Work down this side (9), across the top (10), down the other side (11), and finally snip the gap between the two holes at the other end (12).

13–16. Now use a similar action to cut the remaining 4-needle grid to crosses. Snip between two holes on one side of the square (13), turn the paper through 90° and snip between the two holes on the next side (14), turn the paper again and snip the third side (15), and finally turn it once more and snip the fourth side (16).

Finishing off the card

You can simply fold the embossed parchment paper to make it into a card but you can also make the card more interesting by sewing in a coloured insert.

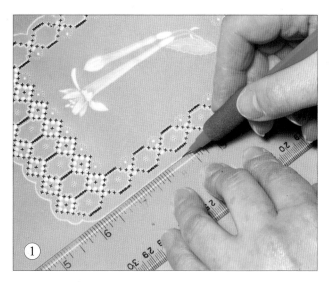

1. Working on the back of the design, use a ruler and the stylus tool to gently emboss the fold line.

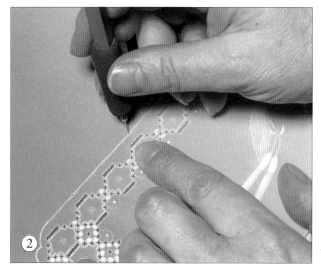

2. Turn the embossed design over and place a suitable insert paper underneath. Starting at the middle of the fold line, use the 1-needle tool to pierce three evenly-spaced holes along the fold line.

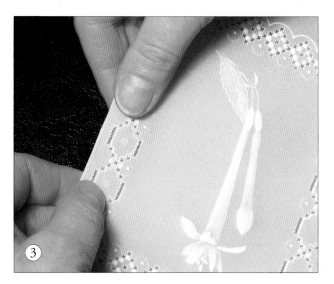

3. Separate the two sheets of paper and fold them so that the three holes stay on the fold line. Define the fold edge on the parchment paper by gently pinching it between fingers and thumbs.

4. Thread a needle with decorative thread. From the inside, pass the needle out through the middle hole, in through the bottom one, out through the top one and then back through the middle hole. Tie a neat knot on the inside.

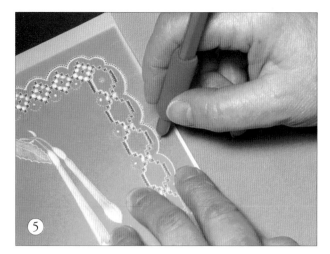

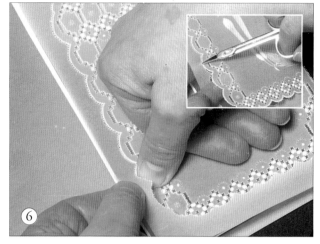

5. Using the 2-needle tool, perforate round the outside edge of the card taking the points through all four layers of paper.

6. Press a thumbnail over the perforated edge and gently strip off the outside of the top layer of paper. Cut away parts that do not tear easily. Finish by tearing away the outside pieces of the other layers.

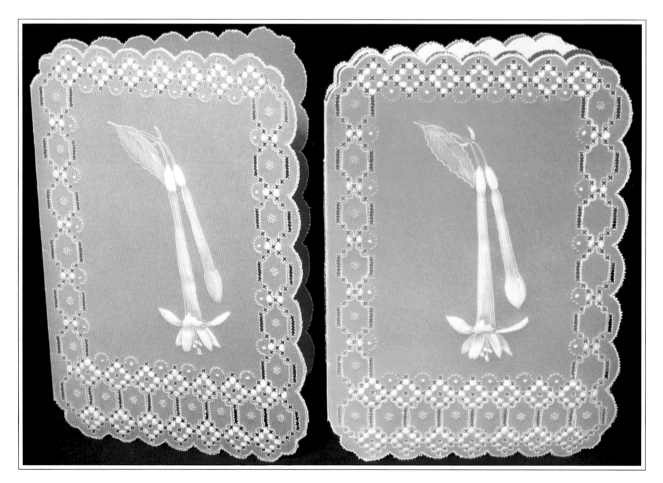

The finished fuchsia design, on its own and with a sewn-in coloured insert.

*Here is the hibiscus embossed within the border design and made into a card
with a graduated paper insert. Note that the whitest parts are the curves on the
petals which catch the light. Different coloured inserts produce a variety of effects
and I suggest you try several colours behind one image to see the differences.
When buying paper for inserts, take a piece of parchment paper with you
because the colours will look completely different behind it.*

Floral-border card

This simple whitework design fits on a folded A5 ($8^1/_4$ x $5^7/_8$in) sheet of paper. Use a white pencil to mark the fold line, then use white ink to trace the whole of the design.

Fold line

Full-size pattern.

The finished card.

Embossing

Use the 1.5mm embossing tool to emboss the petals
of all the flowers and the two buds. Do not emboss
the centres of the flowers in the middle of the design,
nor any of the leaves.

Perforating

Use the needle tool, pierce the centres of the flowers
in the border.

Finishing off

Fold the card and sew in the insert of your choice.

Floral fan card

Cards do not have to be rectangular in shape so long as there is one straight edge to provide a fold. This fan design sits very well on a scalloped border. Mark the fold line and outer border with white pencil. Use white ink to trace the fan but do not trace the crosshatching shown on one of the fan segments, nor the end of the tassel.

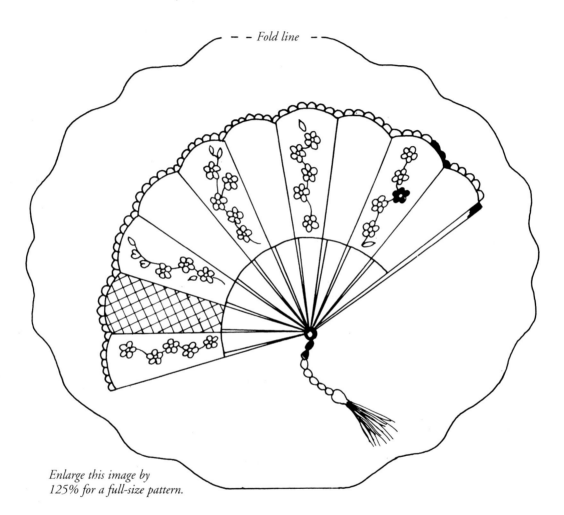

Enlarge this image by 125% for a full-size pattern.

Embossing

Use the 1.5mm embossing tool to emboss the flower petals, the scalloped top edge of the fan, the fan sticks and the ring hinge. Emboss round just the outer edges of the tassel cord, then fully emboss the head of the tassel. Use the single-needle tool and a ruler to draw the crosshatching in the empty sections. Draw the tassel ends freehand with the single-needle tool.

TIP: Crosshatching

The markings on a transparent ruler will help you keep the crosshatched lines at the same distance from each other.

The finished card.

Perforating

Pierce a hole in the middle of each embossed scallop on the top edge of the fan, in the middle of each flower, and in the middle of the ring hinge. Also pierce a hole where the lines in the crosshatching intersect.

Finishing off

Fold the card in half and sew in the insert. Then, perforate round the scalloped edge with the single-or two-needle tool, going through all four layers of paper, and then remove waste parchment and insert paper.

Pansy bookmark

You can use your new found skills to make lovely bookmarks. Referring to the finished bookmark, use gold ink to trace and paint the curved arms of the design, and to trace the tiny centres in the flowers. Trace the rest of the design (except the veins in the leaves) in white ink.

Embossing

Use the 3mm embossing tool to emboss all the gold and white curved arms, and the top four petals of each pansy. Use the rounded handle end of the tool to emboss the leaves at each end of the bookmark, then the 3mm ball to emboss the scrolled ends of the top leaves.

Use the single-needle tool to emboss fine lines on the bottom petals of each pansy – start at the lower edge and work towards the centre taking the lines no more than half way up each petal. Use the same tool to draw the veins on the four leaves and to draw three lines on each fully embossed pansy petal, working from the middle towards the outer edge. Use the 1.5mm tool to emboss the centres of the flowers.

Finishing off

Use the single- or two-needle tool to perforate round the outside edge of the bookmark. Remove the waste paper and slip it into a ready-made bookmark sleeve.

Full-size pattern.

Lacy bookmark

I have worked this design as a rectangle, and have embellished it with gold ink. However you could work entirely in white, and perforate round the outer edges of the leaves as with the pansy bookmark opposite. Mark the outside edges of the bookmark with white pencil and a ruler. Trace the three leaves that protrude from each side of the flower in gold; trace the flowers themselves in white.

Perforating

Mark the four-needle grid.

Embossing

Use a 1.5mm tool to emboss the pattern in the lace grid and the flower centres. Use the single-needle tool to create texture on the flower petal and to draw veins on the leaves.

Cutting

Reperforate the four-needle grid and cut to crosses.

Finishing off

Cut round the outside edge of the bookmark and slip it into a ready-made bought bookmark sleeve.

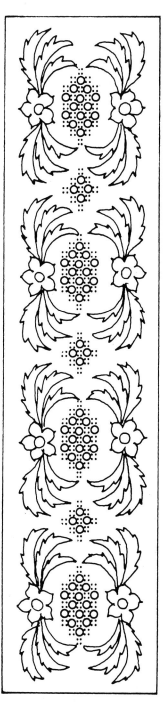

Full-size pattern.

Chinese New Year card

I chose to design a card for the Chinese New Year as a way of saying thank you to my five sleeping partners – my Shih Tzu dogs. You can of course omit the ideograph, which reads Kung Hay Fat Choy (loosely translated as Happy New Year), and use either a monogram or a small design of your own choice.

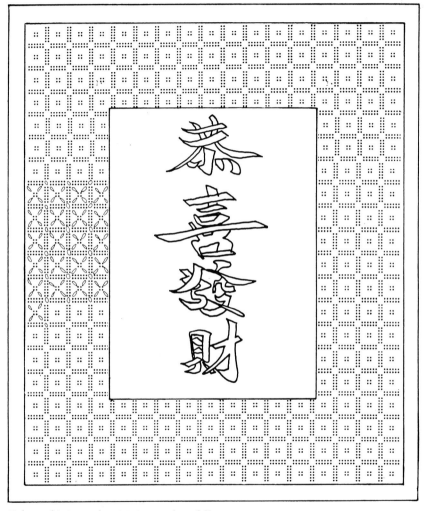

Enlarge this image by 133% to make a full-size pattern.

Colouring the design

Trace the double outline, the inner border line and the greeting in gold ink. Use a brush to fill the space between the double outline with gold ink. Colour the area of the perforation grid with red oil pastel.

Perforating and embossing

Mark the four-needle grid. Emboss the gold outer border, the greeting and the pattern in the lace grid. Reperforate the grid and cut to slots and crosses.

The finished card.

Finishing off

Fold the card and sew in the red insert with gold
thread, then trim the edge of the card.

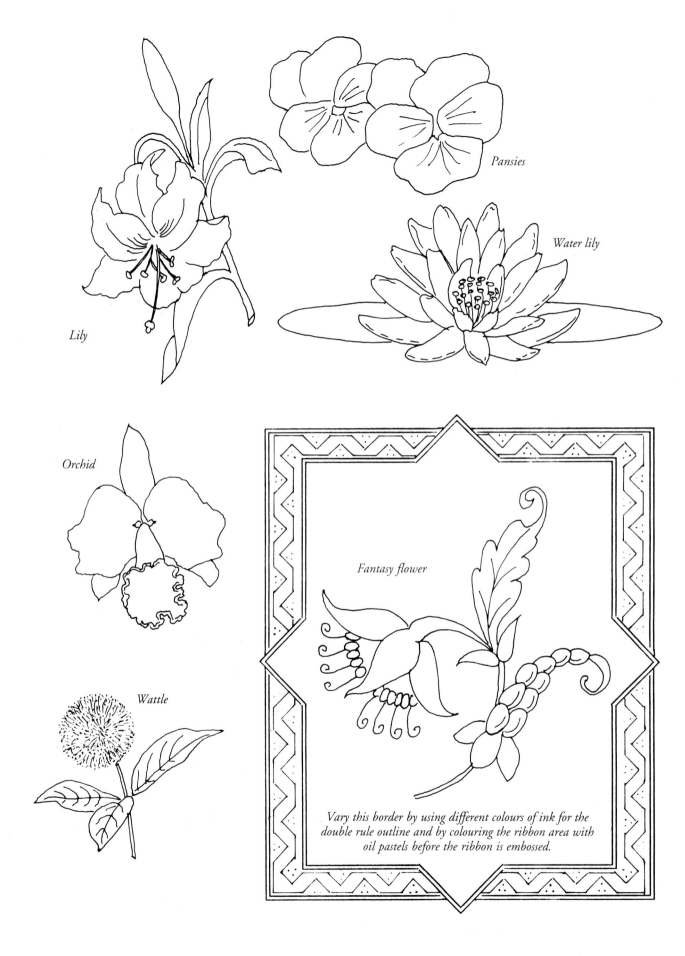

Pansies

Water lily

Lily

Orchid

Fantasy flower

Wattle

Vary this border by using different colours of ink for the double rule outline and by colouring the ribbon area with oil pastels before the ribbon is embossed.

Using oil pastels and watercolour pencils

Oil pastel and watercolour pencil colouring is the simplest method of adding colour, and it is also my favourite technique. Beautiful effects can be achieved easily, and carefully chosen colours will complement delicate lace borders and white embossed designs. In this chapter I show you how to use oil pastels and watercolour pencils to colour the fantasy flower pattern. A border, traced with gold acrylic ink, is also included.

Materials

Oil pastels   There are many brands of oil pastels available and it is advisable to buy a box that contains four or five shades of each colour. Reds, blues, yellows and greens are ideal for flower designs, and darker shades are useful when building up layers of colour. Some oil pastels tend to crumble during the colouring process, resulting in a powdery residue falling on to your work – keep some paper on your work surface, away from your parchment design, and regularly tap the design on it to remove the excess oil pastel.

Blend the oil pastel colours into each other with a small amount of medium. Everyone has their own favourite medium – I use a colourless barbecue igniter, which is virtually odour-free, but you can also use white spirit. Make sure you work in an well-ventilated room and do not smoke.

Pearlised oil pastels are available in a good range of colours. I apply them to the design after the em-bossing process, using a piece of dry kitchen paper or the tip of my finger. Unlike other oil pastels, they are not spread with a medium. I have used pearlised oil pastels on the petals of the water lily (see page 40).

Watercolour pencils   I use these with oil pastels to add shape and form. I work the darker shades of the pencils into the coloured design to add depth and tone and to give a more realistic, three-dimensional feel to the image. There are many makes of watercolour pencil, all with different qualities, so try some out before purchasing a whole set.

Acrylic inks   When using oil pastels I trace the pattern with antelope brown or sepia ink. The traced lines then blend into the colours in the main design, complementing shades and tones.

I also use gold ink for decoration. The technique for tracing with gold ink is slightly different to the method shown on page 14. I use a steel-nibbed pen, and stir up the ink before filling the reservoir. This ensures that the suspension mixes with the gold powder. The effects of this ink on white and coloured designs are lovely. Borders, edges and images are enhanced, even with just a tiny touch of gold.

Colouring the design

First, trace the flower design on to the parchment, using antelope brown or sepia acrylic ink.

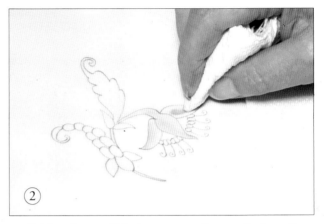

1. Choose three shades of the same colour for the main petals. Turn the paper over to the wrong side and apply the middle shade to the petal centres.

2. Fold a sheet of kitchen paper diagonally into four to make a point. Moisten the tip with medium and work the colour to the outer edges of the petals.

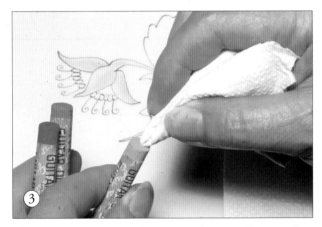

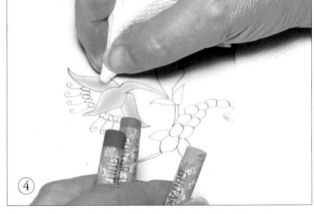

3. Turn the paper to the right side. Use the tip of the kitchen paper moistened with medium to apply the palest shade in areas that catch the light. Work carefully, blending the colour out towards the edges.

4. Apply the darkest shade, gently blending the two colours together, increasing the intensity of colour and adding form.

TIP: Applying oil pastels

- For an even colour, use clean, dry kitchen paper to remove excess medium and oil pastel.
- Wipe away mistakes with clean kitchen paper moistened with medium.

- For small areas, take the colour from the pastel with the paper point and apply to the design.
- Make a new point on the kitchen paper for each colour you use.

5. Fill in the rest of the flower with the oil pastels. To make it more realistic, and to give an impression of depth and form, add shading.

6. Work the darker areas with watercolour pencils. Choose colours to complement the oil pastels already used. Work over the base colour, lightly feathering the edge of the petals to create depth.

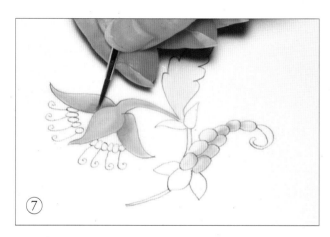

7. Gently paint into the colour using a damp paint brush to add definition. Spread the colour into the petals, deepening the tones on the tips and edges.

8. Continue in the same way on the other areas of the design until you have completed the whole flower.

TIP: Using watercolour pencils

- Sharpen watercolour pencils with a craft knife. Pencil sharpeners will break their fragile leads.
- To erase lines where the colour has been applied too vigorously, simply blend the colours using clean kitchen paper moistened with medium.
- Do not take the colour from the tip of the watercolour pencils with a wet paint brush. The water may leak from the brush into the pencil and destroy the lead.

- Use a shader brush (a small flat brush) for shading and deepening tones.
- Always apply the pencil to the paper first, then work over the area with a wet brush.
- Use tiny, circular brush strokes within the traced lines. This produces a lovely shaded area which will blend into the background colours.
- Practise the techniques on a spare piece of paper before colouring your design.

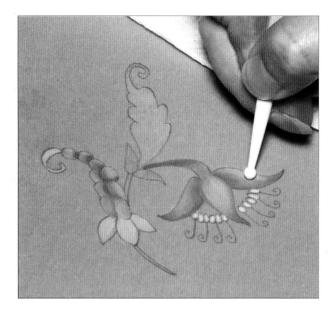

Embossing the design

Embossing an oil pastel design is entirely different to embossing a white or painted pattern. The aim is to achieve texture, not a raised effect. Both sides of the design can be embossed. Turn the design over as you work to check the effects you are getting. It is useful to observe flowers, and to acquaint yourself with the shapes and characteristics of petals, stems and leaves.

The larger embossing heads (4mm and 3mm) give the best results working over oil pastel and watercolour pencil, and the plastic 4mm tool does not leave silvery marks on the surface of the paper. For tiny areas, where petals fold over for example, emboss very gently with the 1.5mm tool. Add veins and fine lines with a 1-needle tool or a stylus on the front of the parchment paper.

With all the embossing tools, gently work over the colour, rubbing the tool from side to side. The paper will take on a textured appearance.

Border design

Place the flower over the border pattern. Draw in the card edges and fold line using white pencil. Trace the border outline with gold ink (see tip below), and the ribbon pattern with white ink.

Using oil pastels, colour the enclosed border area on the back of the paper. Emboss the ribbon first with the 3mm tool to warm up the paper, then with the 1.5mm tool to whiten the design.

TIP: Using metallic inks

Use a steel-nibbed pen for metallic inks – the bowl is larger and holds the weight of metallic ink better than a small mapping nib. If you get a blot, place the edge of a piece of kitchen paper against the blot; when the paper stops absorbing, move to a clean area. Once you have removed most of the excess ink, dab the area with clean pieces of kitchen paper until you are left with a faint gold tinge. Let this dry completely and then gently rub with a soft eraser. You may not be able to get rid of it completely but most of it will disappear.

The lace effect on this border is made with a 3-needle tool. Follow the pattern and mark the surface of the paper with the tool all round the border. You can use the cut-to-crosses technique (see page 22) to make small star shapes as shown in the left of inset opposite. However, if, while the 3-needle tool is fully down, you twist it slightly to the left and right you will create slots rather than holes; these can either be left as they are or cut to make larger shamrock shapes.

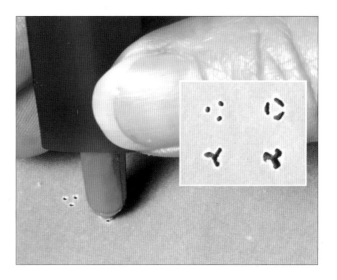

The finished fantasy flower card.

Pansies. Draw the lines on the flower centres with dry watercolour pencils over the oil pastel base. Keep the lines close together and work from the centre outwards to get a random-edged effect.

Lily. Emboss the central vein on each leaf from the front. Keep the dots of colour on the petals small – use a watercolour pencil or apply sepia ink with a spotter brush.

Water lily. Use pearlised oil pastels on the petals to create a translucent effect, and plain oil pastels on the leaf pad. Highlight the centre of the lily with gold acrylic inks.

Orchid. Emboss the trumpet and the frilled edge of the throat from the back of the paper. Do not emboss the petals right up to their edges.

Wattle. Use a stylus tool to stipple over an oil pastel base on the head of this flower, and then a 1-needle tool to create the hair-like stems on the puff ball.

Fantasy flower. Draw the lines in the flower centres with dry watercolour pencils over an oil pastel base. Keep the lines close together and work outwards from the centre.

Pearlised oil pastels

Pearlised oil pastels produce a sheen that can be used to good effect on the waxlike petals of plants such as water lilies and orchids.

In this example, I traced the petals with white ink and used the white work embossing techniques (see pages 15–18) to produce a lifelike flower. I then wiped a tiny amount of pink pearlised oil pastel over the front of the petals to create a hint of colour.

Water lilies do come in a variety of colours, so you can colour them with ordinary oil pastels and, when you have finished embossing them, use pearlised oil pastels to create a realistic finish. A good gardening book, especially one with painted illustrations rather than photographs, will prove a wonderful reference source.

Wiping a tiny amount of pearlised oil pastel over white work will add realism to the waxlike petals of the water lily.

The finished water lily design in the ribbon border. I created the effect of water in the foreground by blending sea green and blue oil pastels and colouring the area under the lily pad.

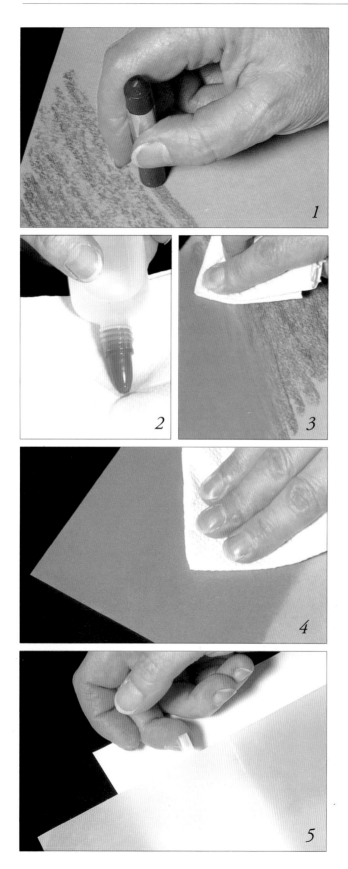

Colouring a complete sheet of parchment paper

1. Turn the paper over so that the smoother side is uppermost, and, using the flat surface of the oil pastel (some have pointed ends), rub the pastel evenly over the paper, working diagonally.

2. Fold a piece of kitchen paper into four and put a couple of drops of medium in the middle. Everyone seems to have their own favourite medium. I prefer to use colourless barbecue igniter, which is virtually odour-free, but some people use white spirit or other art mediums. Whichever medium you choose, please work in an airy room and do not smoke.

3. The next job is to even out the colour and remove the excess pastel. Paler colours can usually be evened out by rubbing the surface with a folded piece of kitchen paper, which will remove the excess pastel and give you an even, pale colour. The darker colours need some medium to spread them. Fold the paper into four again and start wiping it over the paper in the same direction as you applied the pastel. If you have too much medium on the paper you will find that it will wipe the paper clean; too little and it will not spread the pastel evenly.

4. When you have finished, wipe the area of the card with a clean piece of folded kitchen paper. This will remove any excess medium and pastel from the parchment. Also wipe the edges of the parchment paper clean. You should end up with a delicately, evenly coloured piece of paper.

5. Finally, take the paper you have coloured, turn it over, and carefully affix it to the pattern. Be careful where you place the sticky tape as this will remove the colour from your paper.

Then trace the design, remove the paper from the pattern, turn it over, and emboss it in the normal way from the back.

The embossing will show up white on the right side and the overall effect of white tracing and embossing on a coloured background gives a totally different slant to any of the patterns that we have already covered in this book.

Rainbow colouring with oil pastels

This method gives a graded coloured background, so choose colours that blend together well. I am particularly fond of magenta, dark blue and violet. An autumnal combination can be made with brown, yellow and orange; or try green, yellow and brown. Even two different shades of the same colour can look good. Remember that the oil pastel will not be as dark as it appears in the stick once you have spread it on the parchment paper.

I usually work on the diagonal for the best striped effect, but you can work in boxlike squares, starting with a solid middle and adding a border of another colour, followed by a border of a third colour. You could even make it circular, starting with one colour and adding bands of different colours. Whichever you choose, the method is the same.

Start with your first chosen colour and make a band at least 2.5cm (1in) wide. Apply it using the flat end of the pastel; then, leaving a tiny gap, apply a band of the next colour, remembering to make it at least 2.5cm (1in) wide. Next, leaving a tiny gap, apply a band of the third colour. Repeat this process, starting with the first colour again, until you have covered the area you wish to be coloured.

Using your chosen medium on a piece of kitchen paper, spread the bands of the same colour. Change the kitchen paper round to get a clean bit and spread the bands of the second colour. Finally, again changing the kitchen paper round, spread the bands of the third colour. If you do not turn the kitchen paper so that you have a clean piece for each colour, you will transfer one colour on to the next.

Then, again choosing a clean area of the kitchen paper, work the area between the stripes so that they blend one into the other. Here, again, I usually work the stripes of the same colour at one time and then change the kitchen paper round and blend the next sets of areas between the stripes. Once you have finished blending, use a clean piece of dry kitchen paper and rub off any excess medium and colour. Make sure you have a clean area for each stripe and the area where they blend one into the other. You should end up with a delicately coloured rainbow effect.

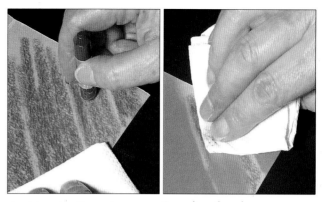

Applying the oil pastel.   *Spreading the colour.*

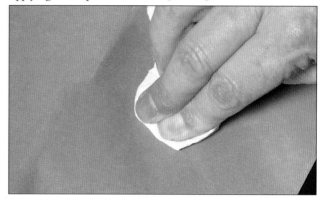

Blending the edges of the stripes.

An alternative way of applying the colour – in squares.

Softening the edges of the squares for a misty effect.

Morning glory card

The flower is cut out so that it overlaps the background. Trace the card edges, and the central and middle fold line, with a white pencil, then trace the flower using sepia ink.

Colouring the design

Colour the flower first, beginning on the back of the design. Using oil pastels, choose two shades of blue and green and apply the darker shades to the petals and leaves. Turn the design over and apply the two colours, working from the palest to the darkest. More definition is required where the petals overlap so

blend in blue watercolour pencil, to deepen the tones. Mark the veins on the leaves with a brown watercolour pencil. Finally add yellow oil pastel to the flower centres.

Embossing the design

Using the plastic headed tool, gently emboss the flower petals in the lightest areas. This will give the petals a slight curve upwards. Turn the design over and use the 1.5mm tool to emboss the yellow centres. Finally, run a line down the centre of each leaf with a 1-needle tool.

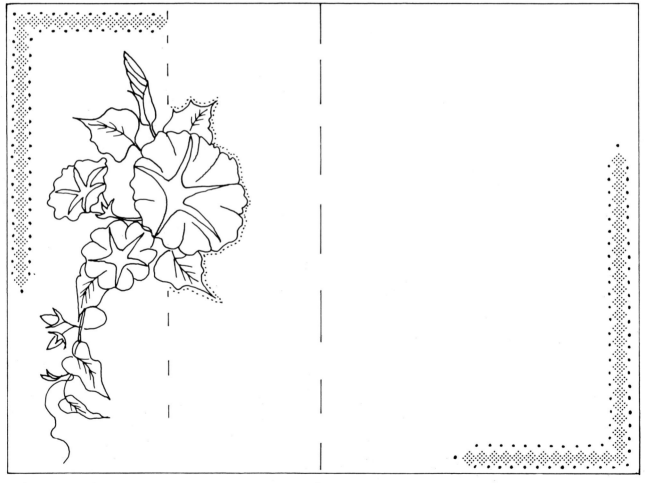

The pattern on this page is reproduced at 80%.
Enlarge by 125% to get a full-size pattern.

Border design

The lace grid round the border forms a diamond pattern. Using the 4-needle tool, gently mark the design on the front of the paper (see Stage 3 on page 20). Working from the back of the picture, emboss the small dots in the lace grid using the stylus.

From the front of the design, re-perforate the 4-needle grid, then cut the central part of each diamond to crosses. Cut around the edge of the card with scissors, then carefully perforate the lines around the overlapping flower and leaves using a single needle tool. Gently cut these perforations with scissors.

On the front of the design, emboss the central fold line with the stylus. Turn the design over and emboss the two short fold lines on the front. Fold the front page back leaving the main flower and leaves flat, then fold the central line inwards to form the card.

The finished card.

Art nouveau lady

Colouring faces is always a problem and many of us, I am sure, will have produced a face that looks as though the subject has a nasty skin problem or needs eye surgery! Here is how to avoid that happening.

Colouring and embossing

Trace flesh outlines, features and hair with sepia ink – black always looks too heavy. Eyebrows are a series of fine lines at a slight angle and lashes are angled towards the outer corner of the eye. Do not emphasize lower lashes; a few very short ones at the outer eye corner edge is enough.

Trace the irises with blue, dark green or brown ink, and remember that they are not completely round as the eyelids hide the top and bottom curves. Use a brush and the same colour ink to fill in each iris. Draw the pupils with black ink and fill them in with a brush. Using a pen, add a highlight dot of white ink to the iris of each eye making sure that it is in the same position in both eyes. Emboss the white of the eye area from the back of the paper.

Use a thin wash of ink (pinky-red, not a vivid shade) to colour the lips and a pale brown oil pastel on the back of the paper for the flesh areas. Add shadows to the face and neck, and a faint blush to the cheeks, using oil pastel on the front of the paper.

For the hair, choose three shades of oil pastel – remember that blondes and redheads both have some brown in their hair. Spread the middle colour oil pastel on the back of the paper, and then use the shading techniques (see page 36) on the front to produce realistic hair. Lightly emboss for texture and add fine flecks with a stylus to give highlights.

For the dress, a mixture of techniques have been used. The white areas are advanced embossing techniques, whilst the jewelled pectoral uses gold ink tracing and felt-tip techniques. The flowers in the hair are pearlised ink and the centres are produced by using bead point (a special material used for painting cross stitch type patterns). Bead point work must be left to dry for at least twenty-four hours.

Working the border

Using gold ink, trace the edges of the card and the double-circle border. Emboss the space between the circles or fill it with oil pastel. Mark the lace grid, emboss the design in the border, re-perforate the lace and cut to crosses.

This pattern is reproduced at 80%.
Enlarge by 125% to get a full-size pattern.

Two versions of the finished picture. On the upper one, I traced the two circles with white ink and coloured the gap between. On the lower one, I coloured the border area between the outer gold circle and the outside edge with a pale blue oil pastel and embossed the gap between the two circles.

Fantasy flowers and butterfly

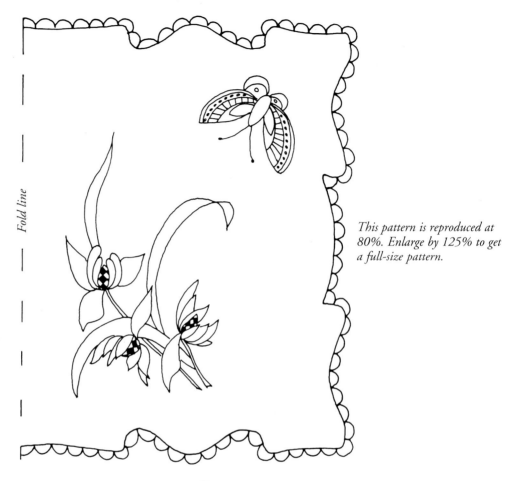

Fold line

This pattern is reproduced at 80%. Enlarge by 125% to get a full-size pattern.

Tracing

Mark the fold line with white pencil and ruler. Use gold ink to trace the dots on the butterfly wings, the two inner eye-shaped areas on the top wings and the two petals either side of the chequerboard centre of each flower. With white ink, trace the rest of the design (not the butterfly feelers) and the border.

Oil pastels

Colour the front page only. Start in the top right-hand corner and make bands of alternating colours at least 2.5cm (1in) wide – approximately five bands of colour in all. Spread the colours and blend the area between the stripes so that one colour blends into the next. Finish off by wiping each area with a clean, dry piece of kitchen paper.

Painting

Using gold ink, fill in the traced outline of the eye shape in the butterfly wings and the two petals on either side of the chequerboard centre of each flower.

Embossing

Emboss the semicircular shapes round the border edge, using the 3mm tool to 'warm' the paper up, and then follow this with the 1.5mm tool to give a really white appearance. Next, emboss between the double outer lines of each butterfly wing and every other stripe in the upper wings. Also emboss the gold-painted eye-shaped areas. The body of the butterfly is gently embossed with the 3mm tool. Freehand emboss in the feelers of the butterfly, using the pattern for guidance. With the stylus, draw a line down the centre of each of the large flower petals on the right side of the paper (this applies to five petals only – see the photograph for guidance), turn the paper over, and emboss the area between the central line and the outside edge of these petals until they are very white.

Emboss the gold-coloured petals and then, with the 3mm tool, the petals on either side of the gold-coloured ones to a pale grey colour. See the photograph for guidance. Emboss the leaves lightly with the 3mm tool and then, using the single-needle tool, draw a line down the centre of each leaf on the right side of the paper. Using the 1mm tool, emboss areas of central petal to give the chequerboard effect.

Finishing off

Fold the card and sew in any insert. Using either the single- or the two-needle tool, perforate round the scalloped edge of the card.

The finished card.

Religious card

There may be times when you want to send a card with a Christian message. For those occasions, such as Easter, a christening, a First Communion, or a wedding, this card will be ideal. It would also be suitable as a condolence card. Add lettering to the card, or change your choice of oil pastel. For example, if you wish to use it as a sympathy card, use lilac or purple oil pastel on the reverse of the paper. For a wedding or christening, you can change the flower design.

This pattern is reproduced at 50%.
Enlarge by 200% to get a full-size pattern.

Tracing

Mark the fold line and the outer edges of the card with a white pencil. Trace the outlines of the double oval and the cross, and the circles within the cross shape with silver ink. Trace the rest of the design in white ink. Fill in the double oval with silver ink.

Oil pastel

On the front of the card, use two shades of green for the lily leaves and yellow for the stamens.

Embossing

Use the single-needle tool and a ruler to crosshatch the cross. Use the 1.5mm tool to emboss the double outline of the cross and the circles within it. Use the 3mm tool to emboss the oval around the cross, then gently emboss the leaves, working at an angle from the outside edge to the middle of the leaf on each side. Gently emboss the lower cup of the lily and the petal edges, then add a bit of extra embossing at the bottom of the cup where it joins the stem to give the effect of light catching it. Use the 1.5mm tool to make petal edges that you started with the 3mm tool very white. Emboss the central stamen, then emboss the turned-over edge on two of the lilies from the *front* of the paper. Now, with the fine point, draw in the central and side veins of the leaves on the *front* of the paper.

The finished card.

Perforating

Use the single-needle tool to pierce a hole at the intersections of the lines in the cross, then to perforate the outline of the cross, taking care to leave four points of contact.

Cutting

Use the parchment scissors to cut through the perforations so that each quarter comes away.

Finishing off

Fold the card and sew in any insert with silver thread.

Oval lace card

Tracing

Mark the fold line and outer edges of the card with the white pencil. Trace the border round the oval and the oval line, the design within the circle, and the circle itself in white ink.

Oil pastels

Using a violet oil pastel, colour the area between the edge of the card and the oval. Using ochre, colour the area inside the circle.

Perforating

Mark the four-hole grid with the four-needle tool.

Embossing

With the 3mm tool, emboss all the scrolls round the oval and also the two leaves attached to each of the corner flowers. Also emboss the bell-like flower heads in the central design.

With the 1.5mm tool, emboss the centres of the four corner flowers and the top of the bell flowers where they join the stalk. Emboss the anthers and one half of the leaves in the central design. Emboss the design in the lace grid. With the stylus tool, draw in fine lines on the edges of the four corner flower petals, working from outside towards the centre, and also on the fluted bottom of each bell flower.

Emboss the rounded top of the bell flower, using the same fine lines but working from the rounded edge towards the centre. Draw in the veins on the leaves of the corner flowers.

Cutting

Reperforate the four-hole grid and cut the sets of two four-hole perforations to slots. Do not cut the four-hole perforation in the centre of each square: these are left uncut as part of the pattern.

Finishing off

Fold the card on the fold line and sew in any insert.

Fold line

*This pattern is reproduced at 66%.
Enlarge by 150% to get a full-size pattern.*

The finished card.

Victorian fuchsias

Fold line

This pattern is reduced in size. Enlarge it to 125% for a full-size pattern.

Tracing

Mark the fold line and outline of the card in white pencil. Use white ink to trace the double border, the square and the circle, and the design within the circle.

Oil pastels

Colour the area of the lace grid within the double border with orange, the area of the square (not the circle) with dark green and the circle with yellow. Choose any combination of three colours that you like; each colour scheme will give the card a different look.

Perforating

Mark the perforation grid.

Embossing

With the 3mm tool, emboss the area within the double outline and the flower-heads in the central design. Use the stylus tool to draw the bell-like flowers in the lace grid and the design around the single four-hole perforations. Also emboss in fine lines on the fluted edges of the central flowers, working from the bottom edge towards the centre

The finished card.

and from the top edge where the flower joins the stalk towards the centre. With the 1mm tool, emboss the anthers in the central design and also the anthers of the flowers in the lace grid. Then, using the 1.5mm tool, fill in the outline of the flowers in the lace grid and emboss the leaves in the central design.

Cutting

Reperforate the lace grid and cut to crosses and corners.

Finishing off

Fold the card on the fold line and sew in the insert of your choice. Trim the card to size.

Mandarin ducks

In China, Mandarin ducks symbolise conjugal fidelity and are often given as wedding presents so it would be appropriate to use this as a wedding card. Begin by marking the outside edge of the card and the fold line with a white pencil and then trace the central design using black ink.

Full-size pattern.

Colouring and embossing

Use cobalt blue oil pastel for the sky area and Prussian blue for the water area. Add colour to the ducks with felt-tips and spread with a damp brush. Use dark blue for the crests; pale pink for the neck feathers; a mixture of dark blue and green for the backs; grey for the chests; yellow for the upright wings; red for the bills; rust for the tails; and pale pink for the underbellies. Add colour to the foliage: use grey-green for the bamboo grass and dark green for the leaves on the water. Emboss the ducks, grasses and leaves.

Border design

Use gold ink for the double border lines (both square and scalloped) and the flowers in the lace grid. Fill in the double outlines of the scalloped central border using a paint brush and gold ink. Mark the lace grid.

Emboss the petals and the dots in the lace grid and the double border areas (both square and scalloped). Reperforate the lace grid and cut to crosses. Finally, cut the edges of the card straight.

The finished Mandarin ducks card.

Three-dimensional objects

Adding a third dimension to parchment work is fun. I use the technique mostly for framed pictures and small boxes but, of course, you can also apply the technique to cards by making extra leaves or petals on spare pieces of paper. Choose foreground shapes that appear to come out of the picture, and play with the arrangement before gluing the pieces in place.

I have chosen one of my favourite flowers, the fuchsia, for the project in this chapter. Fuchsias come in so many different shapes, sizes and colours that I never tire of using them.

The background to the picture is a lace grid arranged round painted stems, leaves and some flower heads. The three-dimensional flowers are painted using the same colours as the flat ones on the background. For each flower you will need one green stamen and six red or purple ones with tiny ends. Buy a bunch of white ones and dip them into ink to colour them – make sure they are dry before you use them.

Making the background

Fix the parchment to the pattern and paint the leaves and stems with acrylic paint or inks. Trace the flowers on the background with very thin red lines. Mark the lace grid. Colour the flowers on the background, on both sides of the paper, with shades of red oil pastel. Use red ink to draw in the stamens and purple ink for the anthers of the shorter stamens. Use watercolour pencils to add shaded areas. Emboss to taste, then re-perforate the lace grid and cut the central grid of each piece to a cross – the rest of each pattern should remain as pricking only.

Detail from the finished picture on page 62, showing the painted and embossed background, the lace grid and the three-dimensional flowers.

TIP: Assembling work

Tweezers are invaluable when putting this sort of work together.

TIP: Removing excess glue

To remove any excess silicone glue, wait until it is fully dry and then gently rub with your finger to peel it off.

TIP: After gluing

Check during the first half hour of drying time to ensure that the pieces have remained in place.

Full-size pattern for the base design and border.

Full-size patterns for the pieces of the flower head.

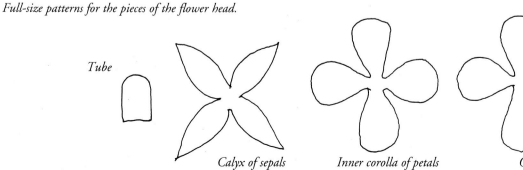

Tube

Calyx of sepals

Inner corolla of petals

Outer corolla of petals

Making the flower heads

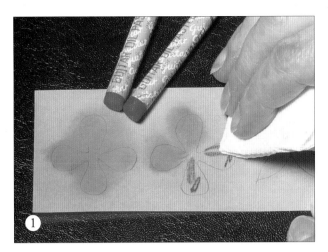

1. Trace the pieces of the flower head (you need three complete heads in all). Colour them, on the back and front of the paper, with shades of red oil pastel. Blend the colour with a piece of kitchen paper.

2. Using a sharp pair of scissors, cut out all the fuchsia pieces.

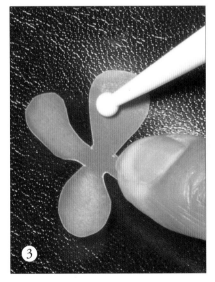

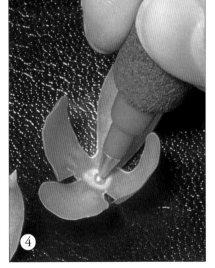

3. Lightly emboss the calyx of sepals and the inner and outer corollas of petals with the 4mm plastic tool until the individual petals start to curl.

4. Emboss the centre of each piece using the 1.5mm tool to make the calyx of sepals and the corollas of petals curl up to the required shape.

5. Make a hole in the centre of each fully embossed piece. Push a stamen through the hole in the inner corolla of petals and, using a cocktail stick, apply glue to the petal and stamen as shown.

6. Slide the outer corolla of petals on to the stamen and, using the blob of glue as a spacer, position it slightly above the inner corolla.

7. Using more small blobs of glue, assemble the calix of sepals. Roll up the tube and glue this so that it is touching the top of the sepals.

8. Add another small blob of glue inside the petals and assemble the rest of the stamens.

9. Glue the completed flower head on to the base design.

The finished three-dimensional fuchsia picture. If your flower heads do not lie exactly as you want them to, carefully cut off the two sepals at the back, glue the trimmed flower head on to the background and then attach the two sepals in the required positions.

Orchid box

Making a box is another wonderful way of using your parchment craft skills. If you can bear to part with it, the recipient will be overjoyed and you can be sure that the box will be kept long after any contents have been discarded.

If you want to design your own box, carefully take apart a favourite container and use this as the basis for a pattern. Always try out new patterns with plain parchment paper; you may have to make minor alterations. When you are happy with the outline pattern, decorate it to your own taste. Remember that the same basic shape can be used many times and can be decorated in different ways.

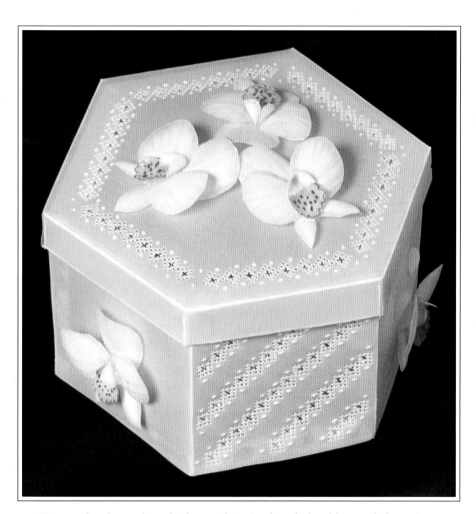

*Try your hand at making this box, with its simple orchid and lace work decorations.
I am indebted to Doug Little for designing the ingenious box shell that fits
together easily and to Marilyn Owen for designing the 'beginners' orchids
which I have used to decorate the box.*

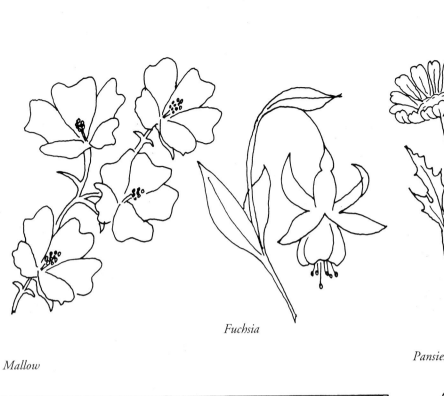

Fuchsia

Daisy

Mallow

Pansies

Fantasy flower

Snake head fritillary

Using inks

Lovely delicate results can be achieved with inks, and they can be mixed with water to create almost transparent washes. Trace flower outlines in the colours they are going to be painted with. If a flower has a white petal then it will not require painting – simply trace in white and then emboss.

Again, I have selected a set of full-size patterns that lend themselves to being coloured with inks. The fritillary is used as the example in this chapter.

Materials

Acrylic inks   It is best to use inks with a stable pigmentation to ensure good results. Clearer and more delicate colours can be created with properly pigmented inks and they can be mixed together to obtain different shades. I use acrylic inks which are available in many different colours.

Pearlised inks   These are very easy to use and I love the soft effects that can be created with them. Usually their colours are so delicate that they can be used directly from the palette.

Colouring the design

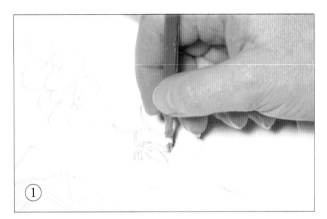

1. Using a pen, trace the flower head with purple lake, and the leaves and stems with olive green.

2. Apply a thin wash of purple lake to the petals.

3. When dry, use a pen to draw the lines that extend from the top to the bottom of the petal.

4. Using undiluted purple lake, add the chequered effect that is unique to this flower.

TIP: Using inks

- Use the side of the brush to lay washes into large areas and the tip for smaller ones.
- Apply wet over dry washes to build up extra colour where you need it. Once the base coat is dry, it acts as a waterproof base for the colours.
- Use undiluted ink, applied with a pen or brush, to add stamens and other details.

5. Make a thin wash of olive green and use this to paint the stems and leaves.

6. Mix some antelope brown to the wash and use this to paint one side of each of the two large leaves.

7. With a pen and undiluted olive green ink, draw in the central veins of the two large leaves.

Embossing the design

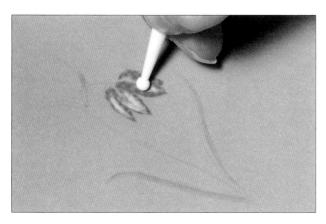

Emboss the central area of the petals using the plastic 4mm tool. Emboss each petal of the fritillary and one side of each of the two large leaves.

The finished snake head fritillary, coloured with inks and embossed.

Border design

Using a white pencil, draw in the card edges and the fold lines around the coloured image, and then mark the corners of the outer double border. Mark the lace grid with a 4-needle tool.

Set a ruler against two corner marks and emboss the outer double border line with a stylus tool. Emboss the curved lines round the lace grid with a stylus.

Reperforate the lace grid, remembering with this type of grid to let the needle travel only about two thirds of its length. With the single needle tool, perforate holes along the inner double border line, starting with the corners. Try to keep the holes as evenly spaced as possible and make sure the needle travels its full length this time. Cut to crosses each of the outer edge 4-needle perforations and then cut to crosses each alternate 4-needle set of holes.

This snakes head fritillary makes a stunningly simple and elegant card.
Carefully select the colour of the paper insert and sew it in with gold thread;
in this example, I used a deep fuchsia colour.

Daisy. Using lots of water and a minimum of green ink, make a very pale green wash. Apply this to the shadow areas of the white petals before embossing them.

Mallow. Use red ink, watered down to a pale pink wash, for the petals. Add more red to the wash for the deeper colour needed for the shadow areas and the red veins on the petals. Use a spotter brush for the line work.

Fuchsia. Mix a little blue with red to obtain the deep pink colour of the sepals. Add more blue for the violet petals.

Fantasy flowers. Outline the petals with blue pearlised ink and then fill them in with a wash made from the same colour. Draw the lines in the centre using a brush or a pen and ink straight from the bottle.

Pansies. Use a yellow base wash for the bottom petals and then add a little red to the wash for the edges of the petals to give them a shaded appearance. Using a spotter brush and neat purple lake ink, add the fine lines radiating out from the centre of each petal.

Snake head fritillary. Create dark and light sides to the strap-like leaves to make the image more interesting.

Islamic card

Using lots of shades of a single colour is very effective on parchment paper.
Blue (always a favourite of parchment crafters) has been used for this card but
it would look just as good in sepia, green or maroon.

Full-size pattern.

Colouring

Mark the card edges and the fold line with white pencil. Trace the whole design in blue ink and paint the circles in the lace grid with pearlised Dutch blue ink. For the rest of the design, water down your ink on the working palette and paint the flowers, leaves, the inner double border, and within the two inner lines of the outer border. You now have a base to work on. If your ink is not heavily pigmented you may have to add another colour wash to achieve a suitable base.

Use undiluted ink to add darker areas. If you are using lightly pigmented ink you may have to use acrylic paint (watered down on the working palette) to add these details. Keep adding coats of ink until you are happy with the dark areas.

Embossing and perforating

Perforate the lace grid. Emboss the painted border areas, the flowers and some of the leaves to taste. Emboss the design in the lace grid and the painted areas of the lace grid. Reperforate the lace grid and cut to slots and crosses. Piercing the central area of each pearlised flower in the grid is optional.

Sew in an insert of your choice, fold the card and cut the edges straight.

The finished Islamic card painted in shades of Dutch blue ink.
It would look equally good in shades of another colour.

Victorian fan card

This is a very special card, reminiscent of the lovely cards of the Victorian era. You can send it folded so that the recipient can fan it out, or you could affix it to a card with silicone glue already fanned out – the choice is yours. You will need to make six fan vanes.

Colouring

Only pearlised inks are used on this project. Trace the flower petals in violet and then fill them in with a brush. Paint the centres of the flowers and the middle of the embossed petals in the lace grid with yellow. Trace and then fill in the leaves with green and then use bronze for the edges of the lace grid area.

Embossing and perforating

Mark the lace grid. Emboss the flower petals with the 1.5mm tool working from the outside edge towards the centre in overlapping strokes. This will mean that the petal edges are slightly raised but the centres remain untouched. Use the stippling technique for the flower centres. Emboss each leaf lightly from the edge towards the central vein and work at an angle to give texture. Emboss the pointed tips with the 1mm tool. From the front of the paper, draw in the veining with the single needle tool. Emboss the design in the lace grid and use the single needle tool and a ruler to draw in the criss-crossed lines.

Reperforate and cut to slots and crosses, then perforate out each vane.

Punch a hole in the bottom of each vane as indicated on the pattern. Use an eyelet tool to fix the bottom of the fan together, or thread a piece of ribbon through the bottom hole.

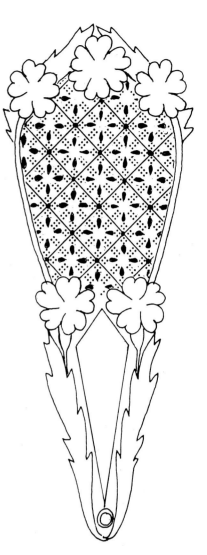

Full-size pattern for fan segment. Make six segments.

*The finished fan.
You could make the fan more personal
by including a short message embossed
in the small areas of the segments
enclosed within the gold border.*

Photograph mount

This pretty mount, in which you can frame your favourite photograph, is
coloured with pearlised and acrylic inks.

*The pattern on this page is reproduced at 80%.
Enlarge by 125% to get a full-size pattern.*

Colouring

Mark the outer edge of the frame with white pencil.
Trace the double outlines of the entwined stems and
the bottom of the flowers with gold ink, and the
stamens with sepia or antelope brown.

Colour the rest of the design with pearlised inks. Use
moon violet to trace and fill in the two large petals on
both sides of the central petal of all flowers; sundown
magenta for the central and two small outer petals on
each flower; a spot of mazuma gold for the anthers at
the top of each stamen; and silver moss for the leaves
and calyx (inside the gold outline).

Embossing and perforating

Mark the lace grid. Emboss the double outlines of the stems and the flower petals, calyx and anthers. Emboss the leaves, working from the outside edge to the central vein on each side so that you end up with a thin line down the centre of each leaf that is not embossed. Reperforate the lace grid and cut to crosses. Secure a piece of coloured paper on the back of the mount with small pieces of double-sided tape (or silicone glue) behind embossed pieces of the design. Perforate out the central area of the frame, going through both layers of paper, and cut round the outer edge of the mount.

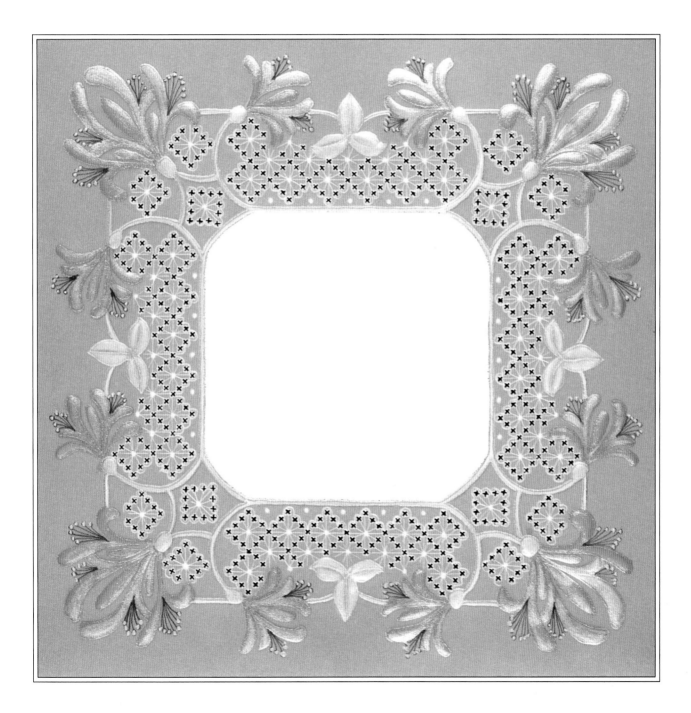

Poppy

Passion flower

Primroses

I have not shown any embossing within the lace grid in this border. It can be embossed and embellished in many ways.

Tiger lily

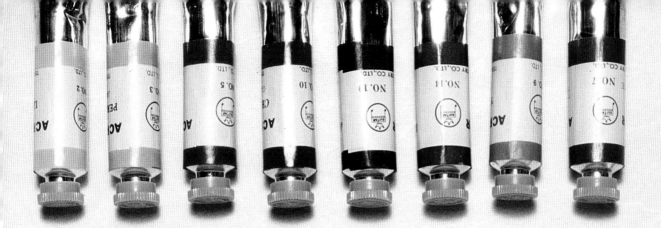

Using acrylic paints

To get the right effect on parchment paper, paints must be transparent, so acrylic paints must be used as dilute washes. Take a little colour from a wet palette and mix washes on a clean white working palette so that you can see the colour you are making; try them out on a spare piece of paper. You may need to add more water (not white) to get a paler shade of colour, or to add just a touch of another colour to get the correct shade. The tiger lily design is used to show the technique.

Materials

Acrylic paints   These usually have a matt finish, but there are several with high gloss effects. I prefer just a hint of shine, but the watercolour technique used does take off the high gloss effect of gloss acrylics.

Wet palette   It is worthwhile investing in a wet palette which will keep your acrylic paints workable for some time; you can even use them the next day depending on how much paint was originally placed on the palette.

Colouring with acrylic paints

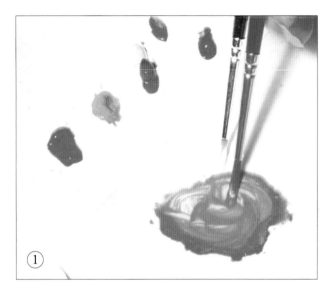

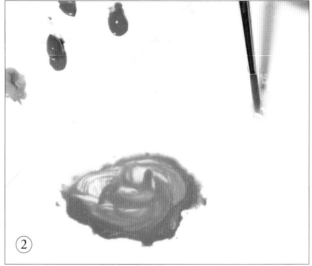

1. Take a little orange paint from the wet palette and mix with water on the working palette to make a thin wash. There is no need to mix colours with white as embossing adds the white to your finished work.

2. If you are using matt paints, place a small amount of gloss medium on to the working palette, pick it up with the brush and then work it into your wash.

3. Pick up the wash with a dryish brush and apply a thin coat to each petal and leaf. This will give you a waterproof base when it is dry. Add successive coats of thinned paint to give transparent shaded effects. Mix colour washes on the working palette. Work using a slight circular motion with the brush.

4. Deepen the shadows on the leaves by adding more colour to the original wash.

5. Add details such as stamens and anthers using a thin brush and neat burnt umber. Outline the petals carefully.

6. Paint the leaves and stem green and then add detail to the leaves.

Embossing the design

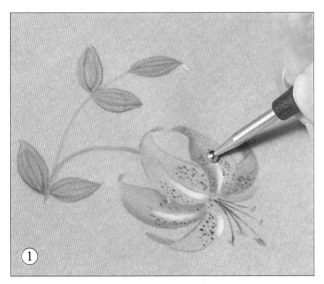

1. Remove the pattern and emboss the central areas of the petals from the front using the 3mm tool.

2. Turn the design over and emboss the back of the flower and leaves using the plastic-headed tool.

Passion flower. The main petals of this design are only faintly coloured so trace the petals with white ink and then use a wash with the merest hint of colour. Add a little more colour to the wash for the shaded areas, and another dash to paint the bud and the main lines in the flower.

Poppy. Use a thin crimson wash for the base of the petals and then add a little more red to the wash to obtain the shading colour. Use a mix of dark and light green together with blue and burnt umber for the leaves.

Primrose. Use a yellow wash, and then add the merest touch of red to give a golden hue for the shading and the tiny lines in the petals.

Tiger lily. When outlining the petals, do not make the lines too heavy; simply define the petal shapes and then shade in using a slightly darker wash.

Border design

The basic border design given on page 76 can be customised in many ways; you can cut all or some of the 4-needle grid to crosses and slots; add some embossed dots; include freehand stylus line work and 3-needle, 7-needle and half-circle tool work. When customising patterns, always try out part of the modified design on spare pieces of paper. Keep these scraps with the pattern for future reference.

The marking stage of lace borders is most important because, if you make a mistake, it is impossible to correct it. Although I am not particularly proud of the border on the card below, I have decided to include it to illustrate how a lapse in concentration can affect the end result – note the uneven slots!

The finished tiger lily in its lace border. I have amended the border design by adding embossed dots, freehand stylus work and some 3- and 7-needle work.

Victorian pansies

This card has a Victorian flavour about it. The oval is attached to the lace background with tiny blobs of silicone glue behind the fancy embossed edge, where they will not show through. Victorian cards were single sheets of card with an embellished design on one side and a handwritten message on the other. To create this effect, simply perforate round the whole of the fancy edge of the lace grid and attach it to a stiff piece of coloured card with silicone glue.

Making the oval element

Trace the fancy border with white ink and the single-line oval with gold.

Using a thin wash of ultramarine and crimson, paint in the upper two petals of each pansy. Use a lemon wash for the other petals and then give them an edge with the first colour, using the brush in a circular motion. Darken the first wash with a little ultramarine and use this to draw in the fine lines.

This pattern for oval element is reproduced at 80%. Enlarge it by 125% to get a full-size pattern.

Mix some red and yellow for the flower centres. Use a thin wash of ultramarine for the forget-me-nots and add a dot of yellow in their centres. Use combinations of dark and light green and burnt umber to paint the leaves and stems. Paint the bow with a mixture of lemon and vermillion, then add more vermillion to the wash for the shaded areas, but do not paint the 'insides' of the bow. Colour the back of the oval with cobalt blue oil pastel.

Emboss the longer segments of the frill from the back of the paper and the shorter ones from the front. Gently emboss the flowers and the bow, working the inside parts of the latter from the front of the paper. Finally, perforate round the frilled edge.

Making the lace background

If you want to produce this design on a folded card, mark the fold line with a white pencil; some of the lace border edge will extend over the fold line.

Trace the outer frilled edge and the central oval in white ink and the double-rule outer border with gold. Mark the lace grid. Emboss the straight lines in the grid using the 1-needle tool and a ruler. Emboss between the double gold lines and the individual segments of the frilled edge.

Reperforate the lace grid (only taking the needle tool two-thirds of its length through the paper) and then cut out the centre four-hole part of each block. Pierce a hole at all intersections of the straight lines. Perforate round the frilled edge. (If you are making a folded card, perforate out the small section of the frilled edge that overhangs the fold line before folding the card.) Finally, attach the completed oval element to the background with tiny blobs of silicone glue.

This pattern for lace grid background is reproduced at 80%. Enlarge it by 125% to get a full-size pattern.

*Here is the finished card. Remember that pansies come in all the colours of the
rainbow. Experiment with other colour combinations on the palette – you will be
amazed at the number of colours you can create from a limited colour range. The
more you practise and experiment, the easier your colour mixing will become.*

By using other flowers in the oval segment you get a completely different look to the overall design as you can see from this poppy. I always paint my flowers first and then add the border. This way, if I do not like the colour or the way I have painted it, I will not have wasted too much time and effort. You can put these rejects to good use by experimenting with different border designs.

The Art of
Stencil Embossing

In historical terms, stencil embossing on paper is a relatively recent innovation, but it does combine two much older art forms – stencilling and embossing.

There is evidence to suggest that stencils were used by the Ancient Egyptians, 4500 years ago. Early Chinese, Greek and Polynesian artists also used stencils, and Buddhist temples have been decorated with them for thousands of years.

In Europe, before the invention of the printing press, stencils were used to produce religious manuscripts. They were also used during the Middle Ages to decorate church walls, floors and furniture.

On the other hand, embossing on paper only became popular during Victorian times when ladies would have a box of extremely ornate writing paper with embossed surrounds, and matching envelopes, which they used to send birthday greetings and thank you letters. Heavily embossed, black-edged stationery was also favoured by the Victorians, as were pastel-coloured wafers that had delicate white raised designs in the centre.

In this section, I show you how to use stencils in a variety of ways to produce many exciting effects. I have also included some finished designs which I hope you will find inspirational. Stencil embossing is very versatile and lends itself to mixing with the other papercrafts in this book.

Materials

Some paper, a stencil, an embossing tool and a source of light are all you need to get you started on stencil embossing. As you get more and more into the craft, you can add other materials and equipment to your tool box.

Paper

You can buy special embossing paper, but there is a whole host of other papers on the market that can be embossed with stencils. My favourite is a textured paper developed for soft pastel artists. This is available in a wide range of pale tints, as well as a full spectrum of darker colours, and reacts very well to embossing tools. I also use good quality note paper, velvet paper (for a softer, subtle effect), metallic art paper and virtually anything else that gives me good results.

Before starting a project, I always test samples of new materials to ensure they are suitable for embossing. Some thin papers, for example, tear easily. On the other hand, it can be difficult to make good clear impressions on thick papers. Some dark colours emboss better than others.

If the paper you want to use for the basic card is difficult to emboss, use a layering technique to complete a project. Emboss your design on to a suitable paper, cut it out and then mount it on to your card paper. Layering can also be used to introduce colour in the form of decorative papers.

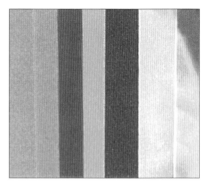

Strong dark colours have their uses, but do test them before starting a project. Some metallic art papers can also be embossed to good effect.

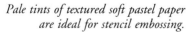

Pale tints of textured soft pastel paper are ideal for stencil embossing.

Embossing tools

Embossing tools are available from good craft shops. Most are double-ended with a different-sized metal embossing tip fitted to each end of a wooden handle. You can also buy plastic tools with large embossing tips. A needle tool is a useful addition to your tool box.

Stencils

Many different types of stencils can be used to emboss paper, and there is a wide range of subjects to choose from.

Brass stencils are designed specifically for paper embossers, but you can emboss through coloured plastic and acetate stencils that are normally used for stencil decoration on walls, fabrics and cakes. Aperture templates (often used for making memory books and other crafts) are useful for creating raised areas in which other motifs can be worked. You can even use the apertures found on some card 'blanks' as embossing stencils.

Some stencils have multiple motifs while others have a complete design. Be selective when choosing your stencils – look at the component parts of each stencil, not just the overall design. You will find that you can mix and match motifs from just a few stencils to build up a whole host of different designs.

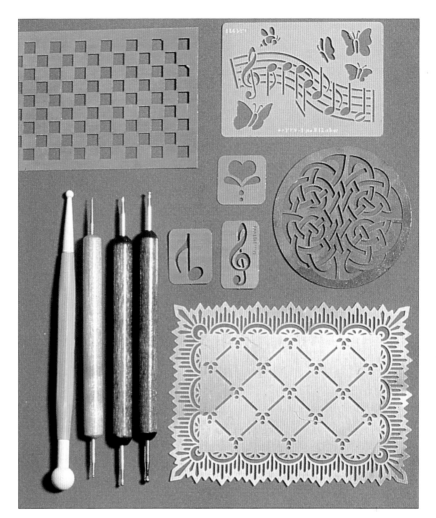

Selection of brass stencils and embossing tools.

Fancy-edged rulers

These are normally used to draw decorative borders, etc. in memory albums, but they can be used to emboss some very interesting designs (see page 112).

Lightbox

Back lighting the stencil, so that its outlines can be seen through the paper, makes embossing on pale, translucent papers very easy. Small portable lightboxes are readily available, and are ideal for the embosser. I do not know what I would do without mine as, apart from embossing and transferring designs on to the card paper, I find it useful for lots of other things.

You could make a lightbox by placing a lamp under a glass-topped table. If you use this method, place a piece of milk glass or a sheet of tracing paper on the table glass. This will diffuse the light and ensure you do not damage your eyesight. During daylight hours, of course, you could use a window as a lightbox.

If you do not have a lightbox, you could use the embossing mat technique (see right). Alternatively, you can tape together two identical stencils, one on top of the other, and slip a piece of card paper between them. Then, using the top stencil as a guide, you emboss the card paper into the bottom stencil and, hey presto, you have a raised image.

Fancy-edged rulers are available in lots of different shapes.

A small portable lightbox makes embossing on pale colours very easy.

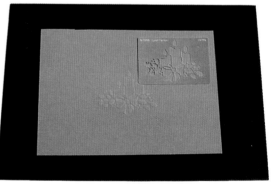

An embossing mat is used to emboss opaque papers.

Embossing mat

A lightbox does not work when embossing opaque papers and metallic surfaces, so another technique must be used. This involves working on a embossing mat, and using a fine embossing tool to lightly impress the outlines of the stencil into the paper. When the paper is turned over, a slightly raised image is revealed – this is then used as a guide to emboss the motif (see page 28). My mat is a piece of high-density foam which has the right amount of 'give' for embossing.

Other equipment

The following is a list of other equipment I use when drawing up plans and assembling the finished pieces.

Craft knife I use this for cutting straight lines and intricate shapes.

Steel-edged ruler A good investment for any craft – the steel protects the straight edge when cutting with a knife.

Cutting mat A self-healing surface on which to cut paper with a craft knife

Pencils I use a graphite pencil with pale coloured papers and a white pencil with dark colours.

Scrap paper For drawing plans.

Set square Ideal for squaring up the edges of the finished cards.

Spray adhesive Use a low-tack adhesive for layering fragile papers, and normal adhesive for others.

Masking tape This is ideal for temporary fixings.

Double-sided sticky tape An alternative to spray adhesive when layering sheets of paper.

Beeswax Use this to grease embossing tools when working on metallic surfaces.

Paper cutting scissors For cutting apertures and masks to embellish embossed designs.

Fancy-edged scissors These are available in a range of designs. I use them to create decorative edges round embossed designs.

Pens I use metallic gel pens to define borders and embossed motifs.

Decorative papers Layered with embossed designs, these add colour and texture to a project.

Dye ink pads These are ideal for creating smooth blocks of colour. They are available in a range of colours and dry very quickly.

Sponge I use this for applying dye ink.

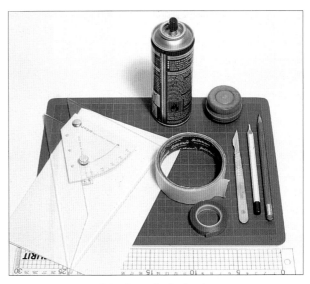

A cutting mat, craft knife, steel-edged ruler, set square, scrap paper, spray adhesive, masking tape, double-sided tape, pencils and a wax pot are all useful additions to the tool box.

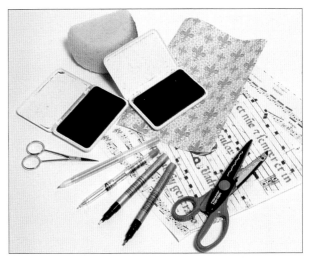

Dye ink pads and a sponge, decorative paper, paper cutting scissors, gel pens and fancy-edged scissors can all be put to good use with embossed motifs.

Embossing pale paper

For this first project, I take you through the stages of creating a folded card that has an embossed design on the front face. First, you should draw up a plan of the intended card. A plan may seem unnecessary when embossing from a single stencil but it is particularly important when you use elements from different stencils to make up a design. Next, you must indicate (but not crease) the intended fold line, make a pencil mark on the inside front cover of the card paper, then transfer the plan to the inside front cover. Embossing the design comes next – do not press too hard or you will tear the paper. Finally, you fold and trim the finished card to size.

Simple folded card

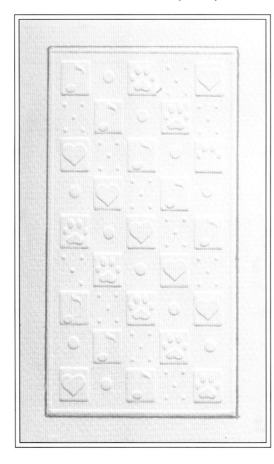

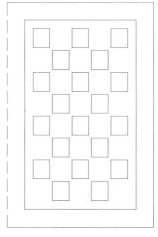

I used three stencils to create this folded card: a grid stencil to create raised squares; a multi-image stencil for the small motifs; and a straight line one for the border. I extended the grid design to give three squares at the bottom to match those at the top. I used a gold gel pen to define the edge of the border.

1. Start the plan by drawing the squares of the grid stencil on to a piece of scrap paper.

2. Realign the stencil over the drawn grid, then pencil in the bottom three squares.

3. Use a straight line stencil to mark the border.

4. Complete the plan by marking the outer edges of the card.

5. Place the card paper face down on the work surface, fold one side over, then make a short crease in the middle of one of the long edges. Use a pencil to lightly mark the inside front of the card.

Cleaning stencils

If you do not clean all traces of pencil lead from the stencils before using them to emboss your design, you will find dirty marks on your embossed paper. Graphite is easily removed with a piece of kitchen paper or a soft cloth.

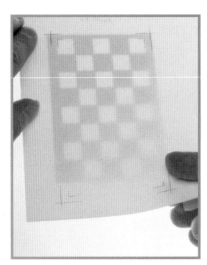

6. Place the plan on a lightbox, locate the card paper (face down) on the plan and align the fold edge. Use a pencil to transfer the plan on to the inside front of the card paper.

7. Secure the grid stencil to the lightbox. Place the front of the card (face down) over the stencil and align the tops of the plan and stencil. Secure the card with masking tape.

8. Gently run a large embossing tool round the outline of each square of the stencil, and notice how each square of paper becomes impressed into the shape of the stencil.

9. Now, using a medium embossing tool, go round all the squares to sharpen up the edges.

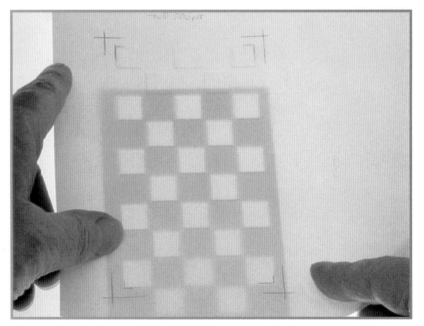

10. Carefully reposition the bottom of the card paper over the stencil, then repeat steps 8–9 for the bottom three squares.

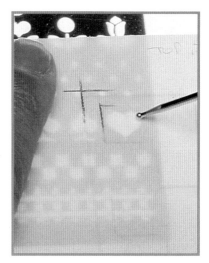

11. Use a straight line stencil and the large embossing tool to create the raised border round the grid design. Take care to align the stencil correctly at the corners.

12. Use the detail stencil to emboss small images on diagonal rows of raised squares. Here, I am embossing a small heart.

13. Emboss the second motif (a paw print) on the raised squares in the next diagonal row.

14. Emboss a third motif (a musical note) on the squares in the next diagonal row. Repeat steps 12–14 until all the raised squares have been embossed.

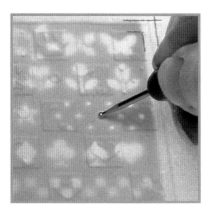

15. Now emboss a diagonal row of five dots in the spaces between the raised squares.

16. Emboss small circles (from one of the flower images) in the next diagonal row. Repeat steps 15–16 until all remaining spaces have been embossed.

17. Place the card (face down) on a cutting mat, align a straight edge along the fold line, then use a fine embossing tool to crease the fold.

18. Fold the card along the crease, then use a set square and a craft knife to trim the folded card to its finished size.

19. Finally, use a gold gel pen to outline the embossed border.

Both of the cards on these pages were embossed from the same three stencils used for the project on pages 10–14.

This design is a simple folded card with a triangular flap attached to the narrow front face.

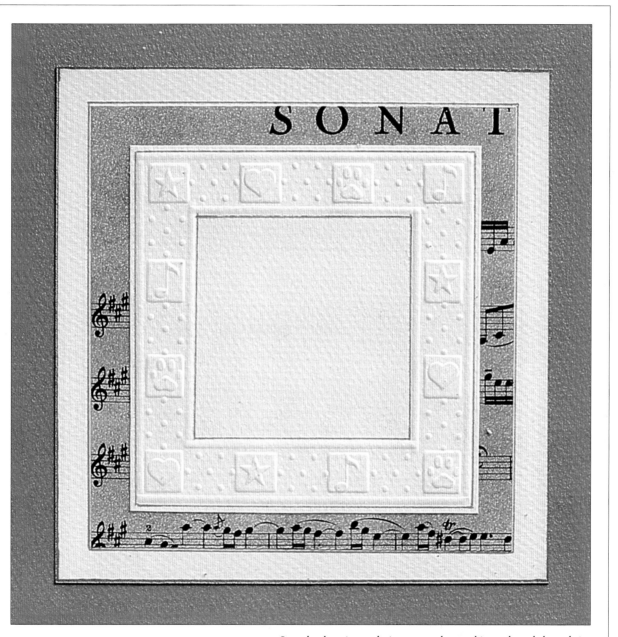

I used a layering technique to make up this card; each layer being 5–10mm (¼–½in) larger all round than the previous one.

The decoration on both cards is cut from a sheet of Italian art paper. Its pattern of musical notes is just one of many lovely designs you can use for embossing projects. The original background colour of this particular paper was cream but, with the aid of a dye ink pad and a sponge (see page 43), I customised it to suit my purpose.

Intaglio images

In the first project all the embossing was from the back of the card paper to produce cameo (raised) designs. However, you can also emboss parts of a design from the front of the card paper to create intaglio (impressed) images. This effect gives a different slant to a simple design and adds texture and dimension. When embossing on the front of the paper you must be careful not to allow the embossing tool to slip off the design and create a mark in the paper. Such a slip does not matter when embossing on the back of the paper as it does not show.

Layered, repeat pattern

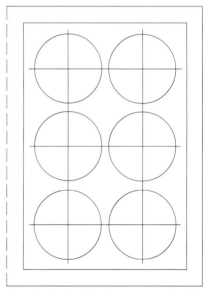

Here, I used a single stencil to create a repeat pattern. For each stencil design, I worked parts of the image from the back of the card paper and others from the front. Notice that I also reversed the embossing on alternate rows. The embossed image is layered on to a contrasting blank card. You could turn this design through 90º and make the fold on the short side.

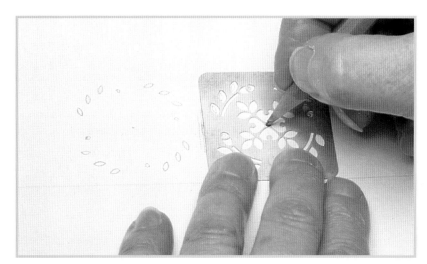

1. Before drawing your plan, try out the stencil on a piece of paper, working some images from the front and some from the back. Decide on which parts of the image you want to appear as cameo or intaglio.

2. Start drawing a plan by tracing the outer part of the stencil and its centre point. Decide on an appropriate space between the motifs, then mark the centre of the second motif. Measure the distance between the centres and use this to complete the plan. Transfer the plan on to the back of the card paper.

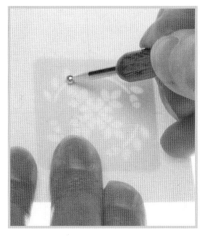

3. Secure the stencil to the lightbox and position the card paper (face up) on the stencil. Use the large embossing tool to start embossing all the intaglio images, then work the same areas with the medium tool to sharpen them up.

4. Remove the card paper, turn the stencil over and secure it to the lightbox. Place the card paper (face down) over the stencil and align the embossed intaglio images with the stencil.

5. Now work all the cameo images using the large and medium embossing tools. Repeat steps 3–5 for the other segments of the design.

6. Draw guide lines to represent the outer edges of the card, then use fancy-edged scissors to create a shaped edge.

7. Use spray adhesive to secure the embossed image on to your card, then carefully run a gold gel pen round its fancy cut edge (letting the pen follow the contours) to emphasise the shape.

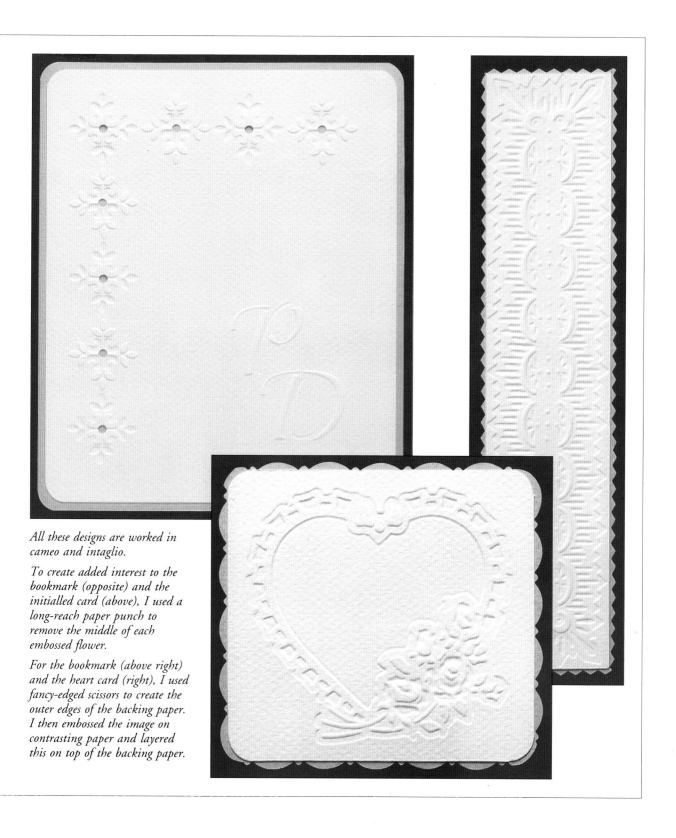

All these designs are worked in cameo and intaglio.

To create added interest to the bookmark (opposite) and the initialled card (above), I used a long-reach paper punch to remove the middle of each embossed flower.

For the bookmark (above right) and the heart card (right), I used fancy-edged scissors to create the outer edges of the backing paper. I then embossed the image on contrasting paper and layered this on top of the backing paper.

Corner borders

There is nothing quite as useful as an embossed border to add dimension to your designs. Many stencils have corner designs which can be extended into complete borders. In this chapter, I have included two projects – the first has a simple, straight line corner border, while the other is more complex. Simple corner borders (with straight lines forming the sides) can be extended to fit any size of plan. However, for more complex borders (with a repeat pattern), you must take care to size the plan accordingly.

Simple corner border

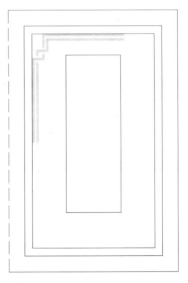

The simple, straight line corner border used for this card can be extended to fit any size of plan. First, I traced round the outside edges of the stencil for the central motif, then developed the rest of the design. When extending straight lines, do not emboss right up to the very end of the cutout, as this may create a sharp edge. Such edges can be difficult to disguise when you come to join up the lines.

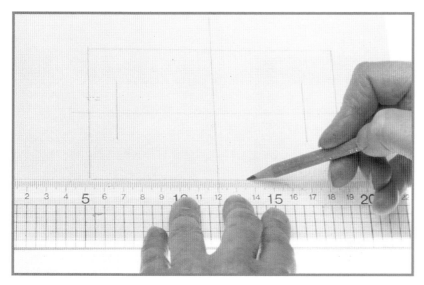

1. Use the stencils to help draw up a plan of the design, then use the lightbox to transfer it on to the back of the card paper.

2. Fix the stencil for the central motif on the lightbox. Align the card paper (face down) over the stencil, then emboss the image.

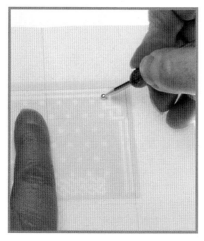

3. Secure the corner stencil to the lightbox, then locate the top right-hand corner of the border over the stencil. Use the large embossing tool to work the corner design, making the sides as long as necessary. Remember not to emboss to the very end of the cutout.

4. Remove the card, turn the stencil over, locate the top left-hand corner of the border over the stencil, using the embossed side lines as guides, then emboss this corner and its extensions.

5. Repeat steps 3–4 for the bottom two corners, then carefully join up the long sides of the border. Cut the embossed sheet to size, then use spray adhesive to layer it on to the contrasting blank card.

Complex border

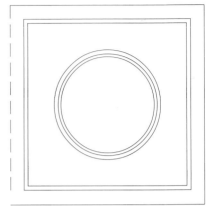

The Celtic corner border selected for this card has a repeat pattern. This type of design can be extended, but you must pencil reference marks through the stencil to arrive at the finished size. You may have to make your design slightly smaller or larger than you intended. I layered the embossed images with a piece of gold metallic paper on to the blank card.

1. Draw a square roughly the size you want the border to be, extending the lines at the corners. Place the stencil exactly over the top right-hand corner of the square, then pencil in a few register marks through the corner of the design.

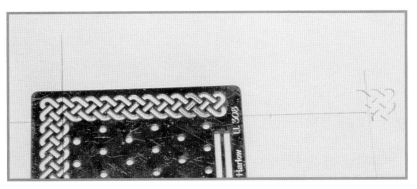

2. Without moving the stencil, make more register marks just short of each end of the design.

3. Turn the stencil round 90º, align it with the top left-hand corner of the square, then check the register marks made in step 2. Unless you have been extremely lucky, they will not match, so realign the stencil to match the register marks (here I decided to make the border slightly smaller than the original).

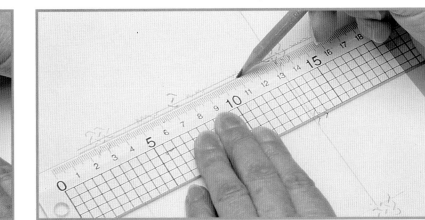

4. Make more register marks at the bottom of the long side.

5. Repeat steps 3–4 for the other two corners. Erase the original lines, then use the register marks to redraw the border on the plan.

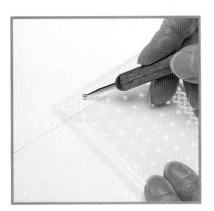

6. Transfer the plan on to the back of the card paper, then emboss the border corner by corner.

7. Carefully cut a circle in the centre of the card. Emboss the central motif, then cut it out. Finally, layer the two embossed images and the gold metallic paper on to the blank card.

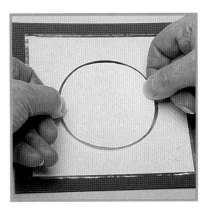

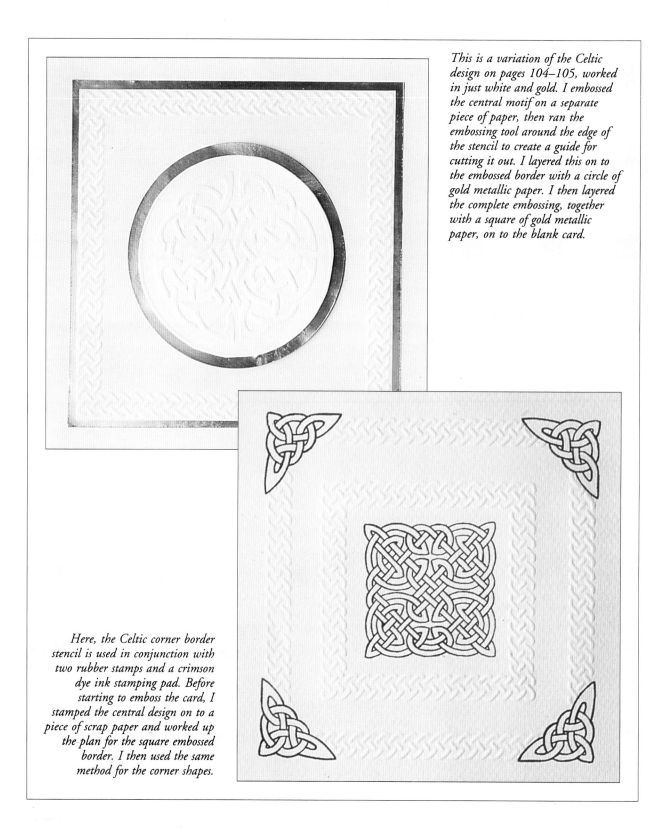

This is a variation of the Celtic design on pages 104–105, worked in just white and gold. I embossed the central motif on a separate piece of paper, then ran the embossing tool around the edge of the stencil to create a guide for cutting it out. I layered this on to the embossed border with a circle of gold metallic paper. I then layered the complete embossing, together with a square of gold metallic paper, on to the blank card.

Here, the Celtic corner border stencil is used in conjunction with two rubber stamps and a crimson dye ink stamping pad. Before starting to emboss the card, I stamped the central design on to a piece of scrap paper and worked up the plan for the square embossed border. I then used the same method for the corner shapes.

Brass stencils are extremely versatile, and I used just two stencils to create this design. The border is embossed from the same corner stencil that was used for the bookmark on page 101. This stencil also includes a lattice design (which I used to emboss the diagonal lines) and a floral motif. I decided to omit these flowers and replaced them with some of the flowers and leaves that appear on the stencil used for the intaglio project (see pages 98–100).

For this card, I used the same straight border stencil from which I created the bookmark on page 100. Here I used it to plan each side of the design, then turned the stencil through 45° to create the corners. The central bird bath was worked as cameo and intaglio to make it more three-dimensional.

Embossing opaque paper

Dark or opaque papers cannot be embossed on a lightbox, so a different embossing technique must be used. The card paper is placed (face up) on an embossing mat and the stencil is secured to the paper with low-tack adhesive. A fine embossing tool is then used to carefully trace the outlines in the stencil and create a slightly raised image on the back of the paper. Leaving the stencil in place, the paper is turned over and you emboss within slightly raised areas.

Repeat opaque design

Only a rough outline plan needs to be made for this type of card. The bamboo images are embossed on opaque paper then cut into strips. These are layered on to a folded card, then the front face is trimmed just short of the right-hand strip. For repeat patterns such as this, fully emboss one segment, reposition the stencil then emboss the next segment. Repeat this process down the length of the paper until the strip is long enough.

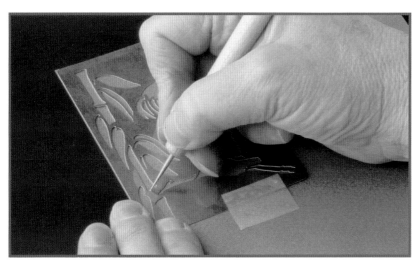

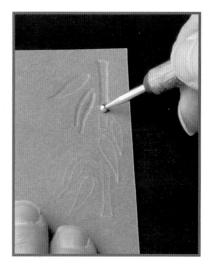

1. Place the opaque paper (face up) on the embossing mat, then secure the bamboo stencil against one edge. Use a fine embossing tool to lightly impress the outline of the design into the paper. Note that to achieve a repeat pattern I do not use the bottom few cutout shapes on the stencil.

2. Leaving the stencil secured to the paper, turn the work over and use a large embossing tool to emboss within the visible raised areas of the motif.

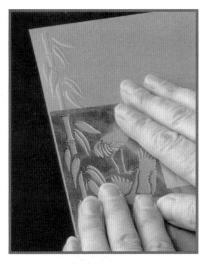

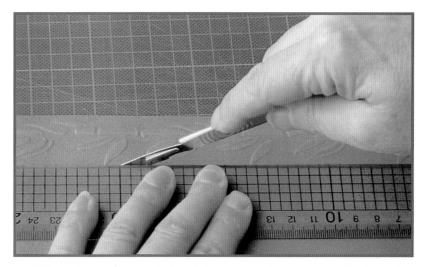

3. Turn the work over again, realign the stencil to extend the design, then repeat steps 1–3 down the length of the paper.

4. When the embossed design is long enough, use a craft knife and a steel-edged ruler to trim the strip to its final width. Repeat steps 1–3 to make the second strip.

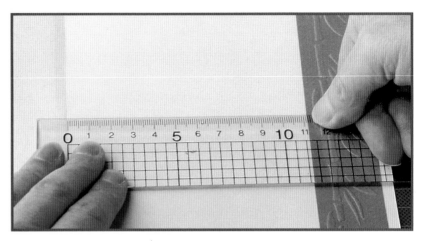

5. Fold the card paper in half, then layer one of the embossed strips to the left-hand side of the front of the card. Use a ruler to align the strip to the fold edge.

6. Open the card, then fix the second blue strip to the right-hand inside face, aligning it against the outside edge of the card. Measure the distance from the fold to the inside edge of the blue strip.

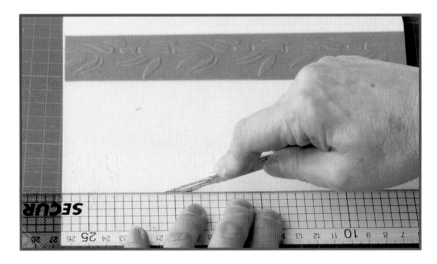

7. Turn the open card over, then cut the front face to the measurement taken in step 6.

8. Use a gold gel pen to draw lines down the sides of each of the two blue strips. Trim off excess paper from the back of the card, then use a set square to trim the top and bottom.

9. Finally, use the lightbox to emboss the birds on to the front face of the card paper.

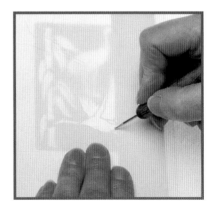

Both of the cards on this page were embossed on gold metallic paper using a single themed stencil that has three images – a Japanese lady, a border and a fan. The embossed images were then layered on to a contrasting card paper. A decorative Italian art paper, with a floral design in complementary colours, was used for the border. A gold pen was used to outline the border.

Metallic paper is fun to use, but you do have to be extra careful when embossing it – it is very thin and can tear if you are too heavy handed. Practise the lighter pressure needed on scrap pieces of metallic paper before working on the actual card.

Fancy-edged rulers

In recent years there has been an upsurge in products aimed specifically for the memory book market. Fancy-edged rulers and aperture templates of all shapes and sizes can be found in many retail outlets. However, you can also use them – either on their own or in conjunction with regular stencils – to produce some really great embossed designs!

Fancy-edged card

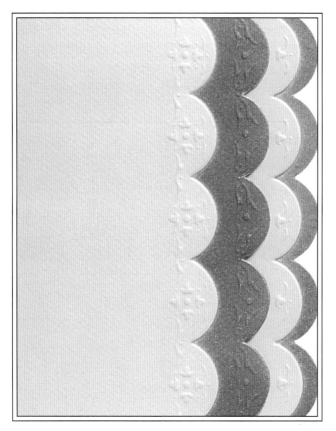

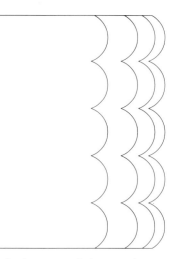

In this last project I show you how effective fancy-edged rulers can be. I also show you how to use a sponge and dye ink pads (normally used by rubber stampers) to introduce colour to an embossed design.

For this design, the front face of the card is cut along the right-hand edge of the wide blue band.

1. Draw a plan of the design and mark the proposed fold edge with a dashed line. Secure the plan (face down) on the lightbox.

2. Place the card paper (face down) over the plan and align its fold edge with the dashed line on the plan. Use the ruler to trace the inner two lines on to the inside front of the card.

3. Turn the card paper over, realign its fold edge with the dashed line on the plan, then transfer the outer two lines on to the back of the card.

4. Remove the plan, then secure the card paper (face up) on the lightbox. Align the ruler against the inner of the two lines on the front of the card and secure with low-tack tape.

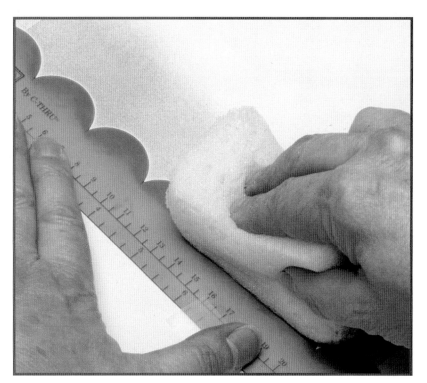

5. Load a sponge with colour by dabbing it several times on the ink pad, then dab the loaded sponge over the exposed edge of the front of the card. Continue loading the sponge and adding colour until you achieve the desired tone.

6. Use a gold gel pen to define the inner edge of colour. Remove the ruler and clean it with a paper tissue. Align it with the line for the outer edge of the card, then define this edge with the gold pen.

7. Cut along the outer edge of the front of the card to leave the gold line. Secure the ruler to the lightbox, place the front of the card (face up) over the ruler and carefully align the inner gold line with the edge of the ruler. Run a large embossing tool along the edge to lower the blue band.

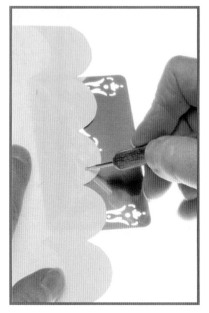

8. Repeat steps 4–7 on the inside back of the card. Fold the card and align the decorative edges, then make a short crease at the top and bottom (you may have to slightly adjust the original fold line). Score and crease the fold, then use a set square to trim the top and bottom of the card.

9. Finally, working from the inside front and then the back of the card, emboss small motifs to both the coloured and plain parts of the card.

The design for this simple yet effective card was created using the same fancy-edged ruler as the project on pages 112–114 in combination with the stencil used for the intaglio project on pages 98–100. Working with the ruler under the front face of the card, I embossed the inner scalloped lines first, moved the ruler back slightly, then embossed the outer lines. I turned the card paper over, then added all the cameo motifs.

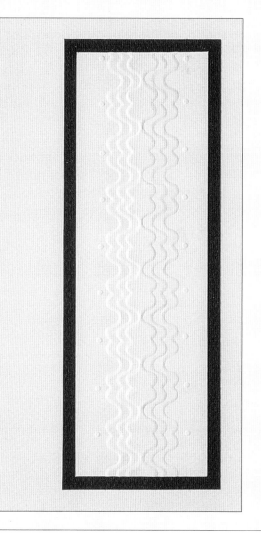

I worked this cameo embossing on a strip of card paper, then layered it with a contrasting plain border. I started by embossing the inner line on one side of the design, then moved the paper slightly to create a multiple image of the ruler edge. I then flipped the ruler over and repeated the embossing on the other side. The addition of small detail motifs adds a touch of elegance.

The Art of
PAPER
PRICKING

I was delighted when I discovered one of the earliest pieces of paper pricking in a London museum. It was an English picture, circa 1780, with an elaborate pin pricked border surrounding a small group of figures. Water-colours were used to delicately colour sections of the border and the faces and hands of the pricked images. I also found an early nine-teenth century pricked mezzotint of an actor.

The clothing on both pictures is pricked in such fine detail that you can actually see the folds and pleats of the material.

Every line is so incredibly neat – it makes me wonder whether the artist used a spiked wheel (roulette), or just a great deal of patience!

In the eighteenth century, Regency ladies added delicate decorative effects to painted costume figures in pattern books, embellishing their designs with pin pricked details and folds. Letters and messages were occasionally pin pricked and sent to friends or relatives. The hey day of this decorative art appears to have been around 1840–1860. A notation attached to a pin pricked portrait of Queen Victoria, reads:

'Pin prick work was an extremely popular female pastime in the early part of the nineteenth century. A considerable amount of skill and planning was needed in its execution'.

Recently, this gentle art has almost disappeared, and I want to revive the technique before it is lost in the mists of time. Most of the designs in this section have been inspired by Victorian cards and pictures, and the decorative techniques of the period.

TOOLS AND MATERIALS

The basic tools and materials required are just paper, a needle and a pricking mat. The other items described here are useful additions to your workbox, and will allow you to create all the designs shown in this section.

Paper

Use sheets of tracing paper to make photocopies of the patterns. This translucent paper allows you to prick a pattern on both sides of a sheet of paper.

Most of the designs in this book are pricked on to art and embossing paper, which is available from craft shops in a good range of colours and sizes. You could also use any good quality note paper. Try pricking scraps of papers that are readily available to you, and determine the type that suits you best. You will find that soft papers do not hold a pricked shape very well, and that thin papers have to be handled with great care.

Foil papers are fun to use and add a modern feel to a pricked design. They are available in different colours and, although they are rather soft and thin, the end results can be exciting.

Coloured embossing paper or card is ideal for backgrounds. Choose colours that complement the design. Make sure the background paper is not too thick if you want to perforate it, or to use fancy-edged scissors to decorate the outer edges.

Needles

Paper quickly blunts needles, so do have a ready supply available. Sharp pointed needles are best. I use just one size of needle, a No. 5 sharp, and I change the hole size by varying the depth of each pierce. Alternatively, use a set of differently sized needles. You can also use special needle tools that have been developed for other paper crafts.

Needle vice

This consists of a small handle that has a screw clamp at one end designed to accept the eye of a needle. Needle vices are available from lace making suppliers. As an alternative to a proper vice, you can fix a needle into a cork.

Pricking mat

You will need a pricking mat, at least 15mm (½in) thick. High-density-foam mats are best, but thick felt will also work. Computer mouse mats are thin, but you could use two – one on top of the other. You could also try using a piece of polystyrene.

Scissors

A pair of cuticle scissors is ideal for cutting out areas of a design.

Pencil and ruler

A soft lead pencil and ruler are used to mark measurements on to paper.

Adhesive tape

Use a low-tack adhesive tape to fix patterns to paper; other types of tape could mark the paper. Recently, I found packs of filing flags at a stationery supplier which can be reused – these are short lengths of tape that have a very low-tack adhesive at one end only. Use double-sided tape to mount designs on to background papers.

Opposite:

1. Foil paper	*7. Scissors*
2. Tracing paper	*8. Papers*
3. Pricking mat	*9. Needle holder*
4. Low-tack tape and flags	*10. Needles*
5. Double-sided tape	*11. Needle vices*
6. Ruler	*12. Needle tools*
	13. Pencil

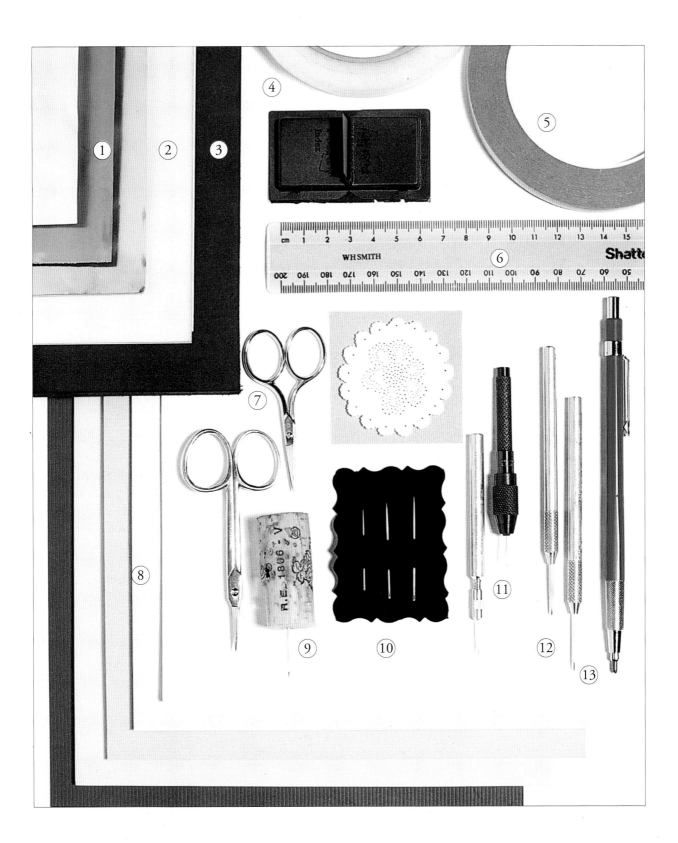

Fancy scissors

Fancy-edge and corner scissors are available from good craft shops. You can use these tools to create decorative borders on background sheets. There are lots of different designs to choose from, and here I show a few examples of cut edges.

There is a knack in using these tools, so practise on scrap paper. Always draw a pencil line round the outer edge of a design, and use this as a guide to cut the fancy edges. Cut up to the end of the fancy shape (the blades should not be allowed to close completely), open the blade fully, align the pattern on the blade to that on the paper and make another cut. Corner scissors usually have a positive stop guide to ensure a perfect cut.

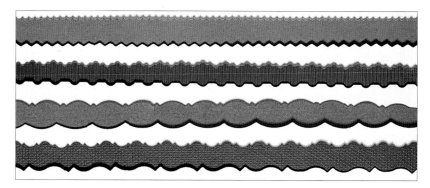

A selection of decorative edges made with fancy scissors.

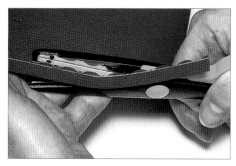

Use a pencil line, drawn on the outside edge of the cut, to act as a guide when cutting edges.

Corner scissors have a stop guide to ensure a perfect cut.

Embossing tools

Designs can be embellished with embossed motifs within enclosed areas of pricking. A wide variety of small brass embossing templates are available in most craft outlets. You do not have to use the whole design – a small flower head, or a simple motif taken from part of the template, can be embossed on to selected areas. Embossing tools are also available from craft outlets.

Brass embossing templates and a typical embossing tool. Notice how I have used just the main part of the butterfly template to emboss the small card.

Victorian scraps

Many of the designs in this section are adorned with scraps, but you could add any decoration – stamping, quilling, pressed flowers, stencilling or any other complementary craft.

Originally, in the early 1800's, black and white scraps were used by German confectioners to decorate small cakes, but they have developed considerably since then. During the hey day of paper pricking, coloured scraps were much in vogue; most Victorian ladies collected them and created wonderful albums. These scraps were découpaged, to decorate the insides of cupboards, to create beautiful boxes and to decorate handmade cards.

For nearly two hundred years now, paper scraps have given much pleasure to craftspeople around the world. I hope they will continue to fascinate us and to be used for many decorative purposes in the years to come.

BASIC TECHNIQUES

Beautiful decorative pictures and cards can be created
with just a few simple techniques – paper pricking,
cutting out and embossing. Designs can then be
embellished with stickers, scraps and ribbons.

Paper pricking

Paper pricking is the art of piercing holes in paper with a needle; a
simple technique, but one that will be improved with a little
practice. Most sharp needles have a point that tapers out to a parallel
shank. It is therefore possible to make different sized holes by varying
the depth of pierce.

Even pricking, where each hole is exactly the same size, and where
the holes are spaced evenly, is best for basic outline work. You can
create different effects by piercing part of a design from front to
back, and part from back to front.

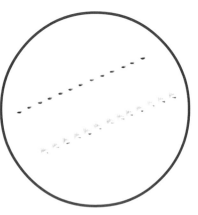

*An enlarged view of even pricking. The
top row is pierced from front to back,
the bottom row from back to front.*

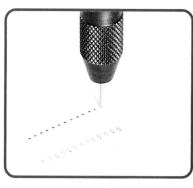

1. Place the paper on a foam
pad. Fit the needle in a needle
vice and clamp it tight. Make
sure that the widest part of the
needle is available for use.

2. Hold the needle vice
vertically and then push the
needle through the paper into
the foam pad, to make a hole
with the widest part of the
needle. Make a row of evenly-
spaced holes, turn the paper
over and then pierce another
row of holes.

Working a design

Practise the even pricking technique on this design. I have colour coded the pattern in red and black. Prick the holes shown in red from the front of the paper, and those in black from the back.

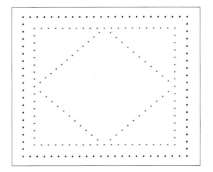

Make a photocopy of this pattern on to tracing paper. Note that red dots will photocopy as black, so mark the front of the design for reference.

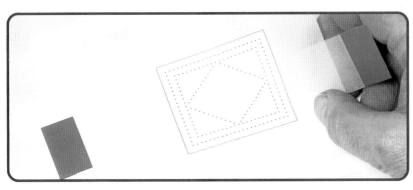

1. Fix the tracing, face down, on the front of a sheet of paper using low-tack filing flags or small rolls of low-tack adhesive tape.

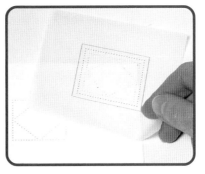

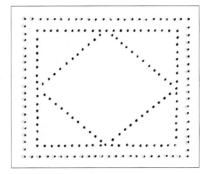

2. Move the work on to the foam mat and pierce all the holes marked in red.

3. Release the tracing and, without turning it over, move it to the back of the pricked paper.

The completed design viewed from the front of the paper.

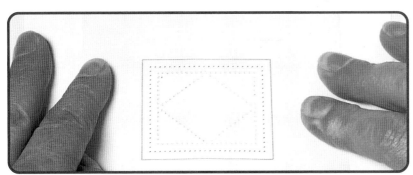

4. Keep the tracing and pricked paper together, turn them over, realign the pattern, then pierce all the holes marked in black.

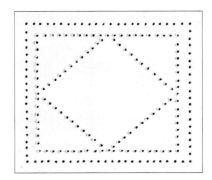

The completed design viewed from the back of the paper.

Varying the hole size

Add more interest to a design by varying some of the hole sizes. The easiest way to change the hole size is to use a different size of needle and push it through to its widest diameter. However, as you become more proficient you will find it more convenient to use one size of needle and to vary the depth of the pierce.

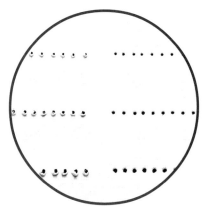

An enlarged view of rows of different sized even pricked holes, pierced from front and back. The top row is made with a No. 9 needle, the middle row with a No. 5 needle and the bottom row with a No. 3 needle.

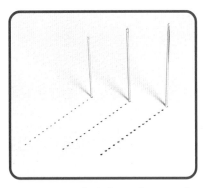

You can vary the hole size by using the even pricking technique with different sized needles. Here, from left to right, are rows of evenly pricked holes made with No. 9, No. 5 and No. 3 needles.

You can also use just one size of needle to make different sized holes by varying the depth of pierce. Here are evenly pricked rows of different sized holes, all made with a No. 5 needle.

Filling in

This is a freestyle technique to produce a tone within a given border. I usually make the holes slightly smaller than those in the main design. Try it on this small leaf design. Prick the red holes from the front and the black ones from the back, then fill in the centre of each leaf. Start with a row of holes across the widest part of the design. Keep the hole spacing as even as possible. On subsequent rows, on either side, gradually change the shape of the line towards that of the outer edge.

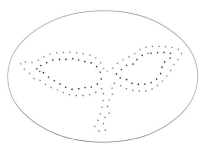

Use the filling in technique to create tone in the enclosed areas of this design.

Start by pricking a row of evenly spaced holes across the widest part of the area to be filled in. Light tones are pricked from the front as shown here, dark ones from the back.

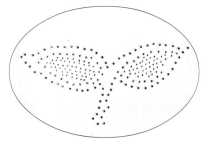

The completed leaf design.

Stippling

This variation of freestyle pricking can be used to create fine texture or a subtle tone to areas of a design. The very tip of the needle is used to mark the surface of the paper – it must not actually pierce through the paper – so this technique is only effective when applied to the front of the work. Work on a hard surface such as a cutting mat; a soft surface under the paper will not produce the correct effect. This small flower head is typical of designs where the stippling technique can be used. For this exercise, use the filling in technique (opposite) to produce a coarse texture in the centre of the flower, then stipple the front of the petals.

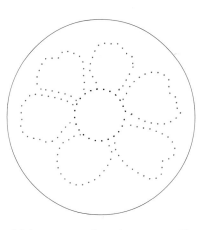

Make a tracing from this pattern. Use even pricking from the front to define the outline of the petals. Move the tracing to the back of the paper and outline the centre of the flower. Remove the tracing and use the filling in and stippling techniques to complete the design.

When filling in a circular area such as the centre of this flower head, prick evenly spaced and even sized holes in concentric circles. Prick from the back of the paper and work from the outer edge inwards.

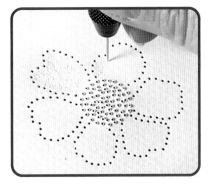

Stipple the petal shapes on the front of the paper. Use just the tip of the needle to mark the surface of the paper. Work across each enclosed area in turn. Notice how the stippled petal has a somewhat concave shape compared to those yet to be worked.

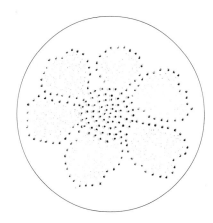

The completed design.

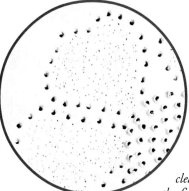

This enlarged view of the design clearly shows the difference between the filling in and stippling techniques.

The flower head in this design is a smaller version of the one on page 125. However, rather than stipple the petals, I used freehand even pricking, on the front and back, to add shape and texture. I also added large diameter holes in the middle of the semicircles that make up the scalloped border.

Cutwork

You can create some very interesting effects by cutting round a pricked border and mounting the design on a dark background. This small pattern, with its scalloped border is a good exercise with which to practise the technique. Always use a pair of sharp, pointed scissors to snip between pairs of holes; it takes a lot of patience, but the result is worth the effort. Do not be tempted to use a craft knife or to tear round the perforations. Cutting will produce too sharp an edge, whilst tearing could damage the design.

When you have completed pricking the design, use a small pair of pointed scissors to snip between pairs of holes round the scalloped border.

The completed design.

Embossing

This is a simple form of decoration that complements paper pricking beautifully. Use it in enclosed areas of a pricked design to add interest. In this exercise I show you how to use a small brass template to emboss an image in a pricked design, and then how to use a needle tool (or blunt-ended needle) to create a frilled border. Remember that you do not have to use all the image on a template. Repeat embossing of just a small motif can be very effective.

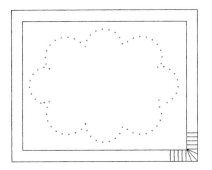

Use this pattern to prick a simple border and then start embossing.

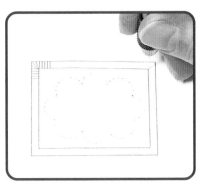

1. Prick the design from the front of the paper. Then, before removing the pattern, prick through all the corners of the inner and outer edges of the borders.

2. Fix a template on to a lightbox or a window with sticky tape.

3. Fix the pricked design, face down, on the template.

4. Use a fine embossing tool to work carefully round the edge of each part of the template.

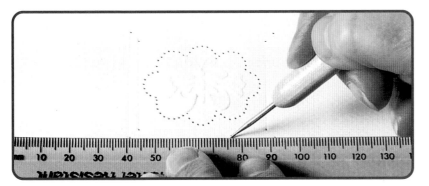

5. Remove the embossed paper from the template. Use a ruler and a fine embossing tool to mark the straight lines between the pricked corners of the inner and outer border. Cut around the outer edge.

6. Use a large diameter needle tool to work around the border, making a series of short grooves square to the edge.

7. Turn the work over and repeat step 6 on this side of the paper to emphasise the frill. Try to emboss between the lines already marked.

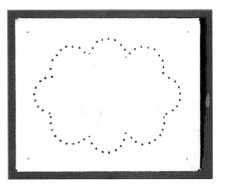

The completed embossed design.

SIMPLE BORDER

This simple border design is ideal for both flat and folded cards. You can embellish the central area with rubber stamping, quilling, pressed flowers, embossing or with a Victorian scrap. The first time I used this design, on the cream card opposite, I found I liked the back as much as the front. The blue card is made using exactly the same pattern by reversing the pricking instructions.

Enlarge this pattern by 125% to make the cards shown opposite. You can prick the whole design from one side of the paper, or prick the red dots from one side and the black ones from the other side.

Photocopy the pattern on to tracing paper. Mark the front and make a note of the colour scheme for the pricking sequence.

Fix the tracing, face down, on the back of the paper and pierce all the holes printed in red. Let the needle travel to its full diameter in each hole.

Reposition the pattern, face up, on the front of the paper and align the holes already pricked. Now pierce all the holes printed in black. Again, let the needle travel to its full diameter in each hole.

Finally, add a little decoration to the central area. I have used floral scraps fixed in place with double-sided tape. Some scraps have a rather coarse outline and I suggest that you tidy up the outer edges with a sharp pair of scissors before positioning them.

If you want to make a folded card, use a tapestry needle and a ruler to score the fold line before you crease it.

These two cards are created from the same pattern. The pricking on the blue card is the reverse of the pricking on the cream card.

FRILLED BORDER

Here is another simple border which includes the techniques
of even pricking from both sides of the paper, filling in and
embossing a decorative frilled border.

*Enlarge this pattern by 125% to make the card shown opposite. The
X's denote the corners of the inner edge of the frilled border. The
shaded areas are those in which I used the filling in technique. If these
areas do not reproduce on the photocopy, add them with a felt-tip pen.*

Photocopy the pattern on to tracing paper.
Make a note of the colour scheme and fix the
tracing, face up, on the front of the paper.

Pierce all the holes printed in black, letting
the needle travel to its full width in each
hole. Make a single hole in the inner corners
of the outer border (marked with an X).

Remove the pattern and then use a
tapestry needle and a ruler to lightly emboss
between the corner holes of the outer border
on the front. Now frill the border on both
sides (see page 127).

Turn the work over and realign the pattern,
face down, on the back of the work. Pierce all
the holes printed in red; again, let the needle
travel to its full width in each hole.

Remove the pattern, turn the work face
up and use the filling-in technique (see page
124) to decorate the shaded areas in each
corner. Work a line of perforations down the
middle of each oval and then work curved
rows on either side.

Finally, decorate the central area with a
design of your choice.

You can also use this pattern to make
different images: change the sequence of
pricking, use the filling technique in other
areas, stipple part of the design or emboss
small motifs between the pricking.

The completed card. Notice how prominent the pricking becomes when mounted on a dark background.

ROMANTIC HEART

This is a simple design, and I have added more interest by varying the size of the holes. The pattern reproduced below is for the design pricked on the cream paper of the card shown opposite. However, you can make a second, larger copy of the pattern and prick the outer border on a contrasting sheet of background paper to create a layered effect.

Enlarge this pattern by 140% for the cream section of the card opposite. Enlarge it by 175% or more for the red background.

Photocopy the pattern on to tracing paper and fix it, face up, on the front of your paper.

Pierce all the holes on the pattern, letting the needle travel to its full width throughout, except for the holes that make up the inner heart shape. Here, to give a little variety, use a smaller diameter needle or limit the travel of your usual one.

Use a large needle to pierce a hole in the middle of each of the small, circular groups of holes.

Use the cutting out technique (see page 126) to snip between the pairs of holes round the outer heart shape and remove the waste paper.

Make a larger version of the pattern – here I enlarged it by 175% – and use this on a contrasting colour paper to pierce the outer scalloped edge. Cut out this shape and add freehand decoration.

Use double-sided tape to stick the cream heart on to the larger red one.

Finally, decorate the central area. I have used a Victorian scrap, but this type of design is typical of those on which you could prick a message. Add the message to the pattern, and then carefully prick round the letters. Make these holes slightly smaller than those pricked on the main design.

The completed card. The red heart is a larger version of the outer edge of the pattern opposite. Remember that when a pattern is reproduced larger than originally intended, the holes will be wider apart. This will not prove a problem on any internal motifs. However, if you want a good cut edge, ignore the hole positions and use the enlarged pattern simply as an outline guide to pierce holes at the normal spacing.

QUILTED CARD

This pretty design combines even pricking on both sides of the paper with simple embossing. The design can be interpreted in several ways and I have included two variations to inspire you.

Follow these instructions to create a card similar to the pink one shown opposite.

Photocopy the pattern on to tracing paper and fix it, face up, on the front of a sheet of paper. Use even pricking to pierce all the holes on the diagonal lines, and those that form the scalloped outline.

Realign the pattern, face down, on the back of the paper and pierce the holes round the two ovals, and the sets of six holes that make the small circles in each diamond shape. Remove and discard the pattern.

Turn the work face down over a template and emboss images on the blank areas of the card (I used two segments of a small flower template).

If you emboss similar motifs, then use a large needle tool to pierce holes in the centre of each embossed shape.

Finally, use round-corner scissors to finish the card. Alternatively, use sharp, pointed scissors to cut between pairs of holes in the scalloped border.

This pattern is reproduced at full size and it was used to create both of the cards opposite. You can decide for yourself which parts of the design to prick from the front and which to prick from the back. Use any small embossing template to fill blank areas.

For this single sheet version of the design, I pricked the pattern on both sides of the paper, embossed motifs taken from segments of a small flower template and then used round-corner scissors to complete the card.

This more detailed version of the quilted card design is worked on white and gold foil papers and then mounted on a pink background.

Here, I pricked the diagonal lines and the two ovals on the front of a sheet of white paper, and just the small circles in the diamond shapes on the back.

I embossed the small images in the diamond shapes using the same template as the one for the plain pink card above. I then used sharp pointed scissors to cut between pairs of holes round the outer of the two ovals.

I positioned the pattern on the front sheet of gold foil and repricked through the outer of the two ovals. I pricked round the scalloped edge and very carefully cut it out. I turned the foil over and embossed images round the scalloped edge.

Finally, I used double-sided sticky tape to assemble the finished card.

VERSATILE BORDER

This is another design that can be pricked and decorated in many ways. You could also cut up copies of the pattern and reassemble the pieces to make a much larger border which could be used as a photograph frame.

Enlarge this pattern by 150% to make the cards shown opposite.

Photocopy the pattern on to tracing paper and fix it, face upwards, on the front of the paper. Pierce the double outline of the central border and the double scalloped edge of the middle border.

Remove the pattern, realign it, face down, on the back of the paper and pierce the scalloped outer edge, together with the three-hole clusters. Discard the pattern.

Lay the work, face down on an embossing mat and run an embossing tool between the double lines of the central border. If you accidentally run over any of the holes in the border, turn the work over and pass the needle through them again. Emboss a small motif in the spaces between the central border and the middle scalloped border.

Finally, cut the paper to size and then add decoration to the middle of the card.

Opposite:

The top card is reproduced at a small scale. I pricked and embossed it exactly as described above. The other card is reproduced at full size, and is a layered version worked on three sheets of paper.

I used the method above to prick the central border on cream paper, and the scalloped borders on pale green paper. I then snipped round the outer edge of the cream paper with a pair of scissors.

I cut a sheet of gold foil paper, following the shape of the innermost scalloped line, and then pricked tiny holes all round the sheet – just in from the edge. Working on the back of the sheet, I embossed small motifs in the blank spaces. I turned the sheet face up and completed the embossing with a very narrow frill (see page 127).

FLORAL BORDER

This decorative oval frame is a very versatile design that can be used in many different ways. On the following pages I have included three variations to inspire you – and I am sure you can think of others. The centre oval can be decorated with a simple scrap as shown opposite, or you can add a pricked floral motif (see pages 140–141) to complement the border.

Photocopy the pattern on to tracing paper and fix it, face downwards, on the back of the paper. Pierce the double lines of the fancy outer border, the single oval in the middle and the small seven-hole clusters.

Remove the tracing and realign it, face up, on the front of the paper. Pierce the four-hole clusters and the four circular groups of holes.

Now work freehand, and add a row of evenly spaced holes between the double lines of the fancy outer border.

Decorate the middle of the design with a suitable Victorian scrap or with another pricked design (see pages 140–141).

Enlarge this pattern by 125% to make the card shown opposite and the variations on pages 140–141.

The completed design worked on a single sheet of card and decorated with a Victorian scrap.

FLORAL MOTIFS

Most of the previous projects have been border designs, so here are two floral motifs you can use as decoration. Their patterns, and those that follow, are drawn in solid lines. By now you should be skilled at pricking evenly-spaced holes – use this skill to prick holes along solid lines. Now you will also be able to make your own patterns from line drawings.

Full size stylised flower pattern.

Stylised flower

This motif is intended to be framed within another pricked design, therefore it should not be too dominant. In addition, the lines on the pattern are quite close together. For these two reasons I suggest that small holes are used – use only half the taper of the needle.

Photocopy the pattern on to tracing paper, fix the tracing, face upwards, on the front of the paper and pierce round the outer of all the double-line work, round the stem and along the vein in the leaf.

Remove the tracing and realign it, face downwards, on the back of the paper. Pierce round the inner of all the double-line work.

The stylised flower fits well in the centre of the floral border design (see page 138–139).

Dog rose

Photocopy the pattern on to tracing paper and fix the tracing, face downwards, on the back of the paper.

Pierce holes round the outline of the leaves and flower stem, in the flower centre, along the curved lines radiating outwards from the flower centre, and round the inner of the three lines that shape the petals – use only half the taper of the needle.

Remove the tracing and realign it, face upwards, on the front of the paper. Pierce holes round the outline of the petals and the central veins on the leaves – let the needle travel its full length. Pierce holes, using only half the taper of the needle, round the inner of the three lines that shape the petals.

Finally, use the filling in technique to add texture to the leaves.

Full size dog rose pattern.

The dog rose motif is worked inside a perforated oval of pink paper which is stuck on to yet another version of the floral border described on pages 138–139. The shape of the fancy edge of the green paper is worked from a 150% enlargement of the border pattern.

WREATH BORDERS

Designs such the ones shown here and on the following pages
are ideal as borders for pricked messages. For example, you
could include a few lines of verse, a quote, entwined initials,
or anniversary or birthday details.

Laurel leaf wreath
Enlarge this pattern by 150%.

Floral wreath
Enlarge this pattern by 150%.

These two designs are very similar and they can
both be worked in the same way.

Pierce the outlines of all the leaves, and the
ribbon, from the back of the paper, using only half
the taper of the needle make the holes. If you want
to show the back and front of the ribbon, prick part
of it from the front. Pierce the small flower heads
that are included in the floral wreath design.

Next, pierce the stem from the front of the
paper, limiting the hole size to one quarter of the
taper of the needle.

Complete the wreath design with freehand
pricking along the central vein of each leaf, and any
embellishments you wish to make to the ribbon.
Use the very tip of the needle to just break through
the thickness of the paper to make tiny holes.

Finally, add a message of your choice to the
middle of the wreath. You can leave it as plain
card or mount it on a contrasting background.

Laurel wreath design
pricked round a stylised
initial J. This card is
reproduced at full size.

Floral wreath design surrounding an initial D.
I used the same corner cutter to make the fancy
corners on both the off-white pricked image
and on the dark blue background.

COVER DESIGN

This is the pattern used for the design on pages 116–117. The geometric border can be pricked in a variety of different ways, and the inner floral decoration can be pricked freehand. You can of course omit any part of the design, and work in your own motifs to personalise the border.

Enlarge this image by 120% to make a full size pattern.

PAPER LACE

This type of paper cutting dates from the early 1600's and became very popular in European convents during the 18th century. There, the nuns would spend many hours patiently cutting delicate lace patterns on sheets of parchment or paper – the work is so intricate that it is hard to believe that it was cut by hand. Most religious works had blank centres for the addition of a devotional picture or a verse.

When researching this book I discovered many Victorian valentine cards that appeared to be made using the original painstaking paper lace technique. Imagine my disappointment when I discovered that the backgrounds were actually machine-made blanks.

Victorian ladies bought these blank cards by mail order, then decorated them in their own amazing styles. On some examples, parts of the paper lace had been removed to create different shapes. Others were embellished in a variety of ways: with silk embroideries, painted images, paper scraps or pressed flowers. I do wish these blanks were still available – I could really put them to good use.

My research set me thinking about how I could reproduce my own version of a simple paper lace technique. I eventually developed the method used on the following pages. It is not as intricate as the original art form, but it does have its basic characteristics. In this case, simple is beautiful. I hope you agree, and that you will enjoy creating the following projects.

In addition to your basic paper pricking equipment, you will need translucent paper, a sharp craft knife or scalpel, a tapestry needle and some gold thread.

Tools and materials

You will need translucent, frosted or marbled papers, readily available at stationers or printers. If you want to be really modern, try using translucent rainbow paper. You will also need needles and needle tools, a perforating mat, a large tapestry needle, a sharp craft knife, a cutting mat, some fine gold thread and lots of patience!

SCALLOPED BORDER

In this project I take you, step by step, through the methods used to create paper lace. I then show you how to assemble the finished paper lace on to backing paper.

Enlarge this image by 120% to make a full size pattern.

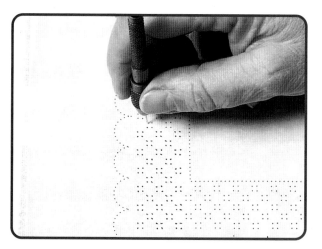

1. Use the basic even pricking technique to pierce full size holes in the four-point clusters and round the inner and outer borders. Remove the tracing.

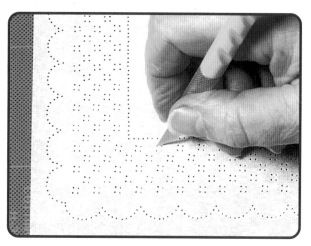

2. Use a sharp craft knife or scalpel to cut between the pairs of holes on opposite sides of each four-hole cluster. Be patient, make neat cuts, and always keep a sharp blade in the knife.

3. Turn the sheet through 90° and repeat step 2 on the other sides of each square. Collect up the small cutouts as you work, or they may interfere with your cutting action.

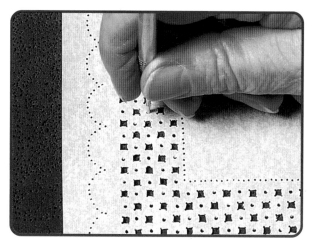

4. Use a large tapestry needle or needle tool to pierce large holes between the cut out squares; these can be omitted, but their inclusion in the pattern will enhance the lace effect.

5. Use the craft knife to cut between the holes of the outer scalloped border.

6. Make a slightly larger version of the pattern and prick a scalloped border on to a piece of coloured background paper. Centre the paper lace image on the background and fix it temporarily with low-tack tape. Carefully pierce through the holes of the central border again to reproduce the same image on the card.

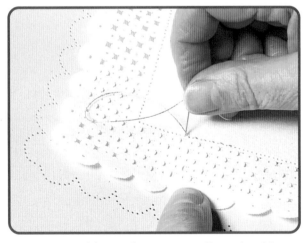

7. Use a suitably sized sewing needle and gold thread to sew the paper lace to the background paper with a simple running stitch. Start in the middle of one short side.

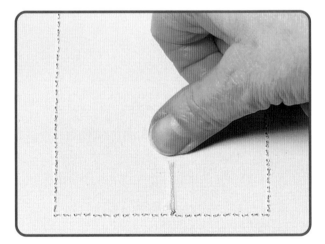

8. Tie a tiny knot with the two ends of the tread at the back of the card, then cover the ends with sticky tape.

The completed paper lace card. Choose a decorative scrap to complement the design, and stick it into position with double-sided sticky tape.

FANCY BORDER

The four-point clusters that make up this paper lace design are cut on the diagonal to form diamond shapes. The fancy outer border and the inner oval one are treated in the same way as the border on the previous project.

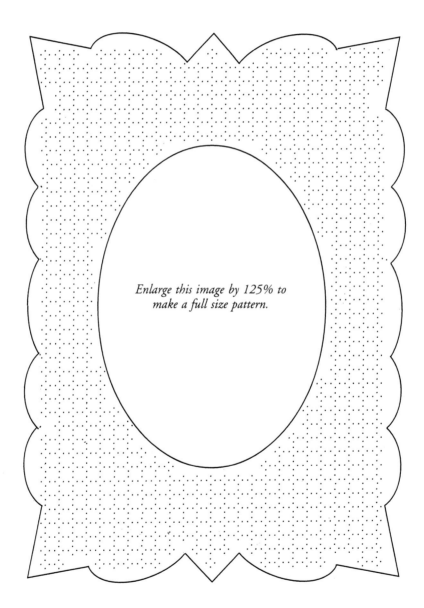

Enlarge this image by 125% to make a full size pattern.

*The completed paper lace border secured to a contrasting
background with gold thread. Notice how the chosen scrap has
been allowed to fall beyond the inner border.*

The Art of
Quilling

It is thought that quilling or, as it is also known, paper filigree, originated during the fifteenth century in the Mediterranean area. The poorer religious houses used gilded paper, probably stripped from the edges of their bibles and missals, to decorate their reliquaries and holy pictures. The paper was probably wound around goose quills – hence the word quilling – to produce rolls, which were then pinched into various shapes. The resulting shapes, when glued together, are reminiscent of gold filigree jewellery.

In the seventeenth century, quilling was used to decorate the walls of people's homes and to reproduce coats of arms. The papers were often coloured by hand before being cut and rolled.

The craft was taken to the New World by the Pilgrim Fathers, and all over America there are examples of candle sconces decorated with quilling, as well as boxes and pictures.

Regency ladies used quilling to decorate their fire screens and cribbage boards. In Victorian times, tea caddies and various pieces of furniture were specially made with recessed panels by cabinet-makers to allow ladies to use them for quilled work.

The paper used in these old pieces was cut by hand, so it is unlikely that the top surface of the finished pieces are completely smooth; they will be slightly uneven due to the fact that it is impossible to cut exactly the same width each time by hand.

The latest revival of this craft was in the 1970s, when people gradually became more aware of what quilling actually was. Papers for quilling now come in a multitude of colours and in a range of different widths – all evenly cut by machine! So all you have to do is roll the paper and enjoy producing your own works of art.

This is a free-standing gilded paper cross which could be used for a small altar in a house or in a Lady chapel.

Opposite

One of the original uses of quilling was to decorate reliquaries and holy pictures. For this holy picture I have reproduced quilling styles used in the late seventeenth and early eighteenth centuries.

Materials and equipment

Very little equipment is actually needed to begin this craft. Listed here are the items that you will require.

Quilling paper

Quilling paper comes in a wide variety of colours. I have found that the most popular with beginners are the packs of rainbow-coloured paper, although you can buy packs with 'family' colours of green, red, etc., which include different shades of the family colour plus a few other colours that blend well with them. There are packs available with three different shades of one colour, which are useful if you are going to embark on a large project. There are also specific assortments, such as Christmas colours, which consist of red, green, white and sometimes gold and silver. Once you become really involved in the craft you may feel the need to buy papers with pearlised or gilded edges too.

Paper for quilling also comes in different widths, but for the beginner I recommend starting with the widely used 3mm (1/8in) paper. Children find that 5mm (3/16in) or 6mm (1/4in) paper is easier to handle when they quill, and this size is also used for making free-standing quilled sculptures or fringed flowers. Paper 7mm (9/32in) or 10mm (3/8in) wide paper is useful for making fringed flowers or leaves as well as free-standing projects. For those who wish to layer their project, i.e. put one set of petals on top of another to give a more realistic effect, 1.5mm (1/16in) or 2mm (3/32in) paper is available.

The most important thing when buying paper is to choose the correct *weight*. If the paper is too thin, i.e. a lightweight paper, then you will find that it will not hold the shape. There is nothing more disappointing for a beginner than to find that what started out as a nice sharp mosaic coil has relaxed into a formless shape before it can be stuck on to the background surface, and many people have been put off the craft for this reason. When you roll a filigree or mosaic shape it should *stay* in that shape, so

remember, if you have problems then perhaps you are using a paper of the incorrect weight.

In Britain and Europe, paper is sold in 45cm (18in) lengths, while in America it is sold in 60cm (24in) lengths. So, if you are making a design taken from an American book and it refers to using half a strip, remember that this is 30cm (12in) and not 22.5cm (9in). Conversely, American readers using European books (including this one) need to remember that half a strip refers to 22.5cm (9in).

Quilling tools

Quilling tools come in all shapes and sizes – plastic tools, metal tools or even just a needle with the top of the eye snipped off. It is important to choose the right one for you and the right one for the job that you want it to do.

If you are just starting this craft, then make sure that your tool will accept at least 7mm–10mm (9/32in–3/8in) wide paper. I have spoken to several people who have been so disappointed that they do not seem to be able to roll the shapes that they have given up the craft. The usual problem I find is that the head of the tool is too *short*. It is only just long enough to take 3mm (1/8in) paper and when the unsuspecting quiller rolls the paper it comes up over the end. You can overcome the problem by putting your finger over the end of the tool while you roll, but be careful, as you can give yourself some nasty paper cuts, which are very painful for a while! At first, it is also best to get a tool that has a collar on it, as this makes it easier to roll the paper evenly. As you progress this will become a natural reaction and you will find that you can roll the paper evenly without the aid of the collar.

Most experienced quillers have a number of tools that they use for specific purposes, so do not discard any tool thinking that you have outgrown it. Keep it – you may be glad of it when you roll such things as roses. Often the beginner's tool gives a larger centre

Quilling paper is available in a multitude of different colours.

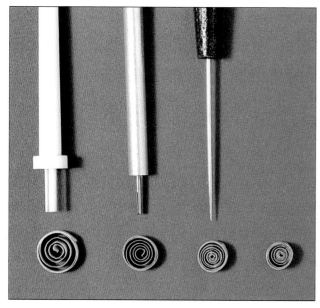

These closed coils show the effects created by using different tools. From the left: plastic beginner's tool with a collar; metal tool, which produces smaller centres; needle tool; and finally, a coil made simply by rolling with the fingers.

to the coil, but again, as you become more experienced you can progress to a narrower tool which will give you a smaller centre.

Malinda Johnson, an American quiller, uses a needle to roll her paper. This is reminiscent of Victorian times, when ladies rolled paper around a hat-pin. The needle tool can be difficult to use, although it does seem to be the best one for rolling spirals.

Some people use no tools at all but simply roll the paper in their fingers. There is an art to rolling without a tool, but however much I try I cannot

seem to get it right! Trees Tra, a well-known Dutch quiller and a good friend, spent a long time patiently trying to teach me to roll paper without the use of a tool, but to no avail – I still ended up with a mangled piece of paper. So, if you can roll paper without the use of a tool, wonderful – if not, then be like me and use a quilling tool.

Glue

The best glue to use is PVA or school glue. This is a water-based glue and it dries clear. Put a little glue into a small container – I usually use an empty individual cream carton, such as you get with a cup of coffee at a self-service café. Once you have finished you can then just throw the whole thing away.

Use a wooden cocktail stick to apply glue to the end of the rolled quilling paper – you only need a little bit to glue the coil closed. I usually keep an old teacloth on my knee, which I use to wipe my fingers on from time to time.

If you want to stick your quilling on to a shiny surface, then you will need to use an all-purpose glue, as PVA glue will not create a lasting adherence. Be careful, as some of these glues produce 'strings' which can spoil your work. There are some American glues which look like PVA but are actually all-purpose glues. These work very well and they dry clear.

Key

1. Quilling ruler
2. Lengths of paper
3. Backing paper/card
4. Blank cards
5. Glue
6. Double-sided sticky tape
7. Tweezers
8. Scissors
9. Quilling board
10. Grid
11. Baking parchment
12. Beginner's tool
13. Standard tool
14. Needle tool
15. Pins
16. Designer board
17. Crimping tool

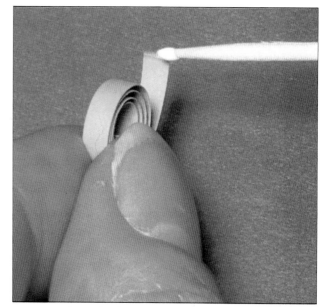

Use a wooden cocktail stick to apply glue to the end of the coil.

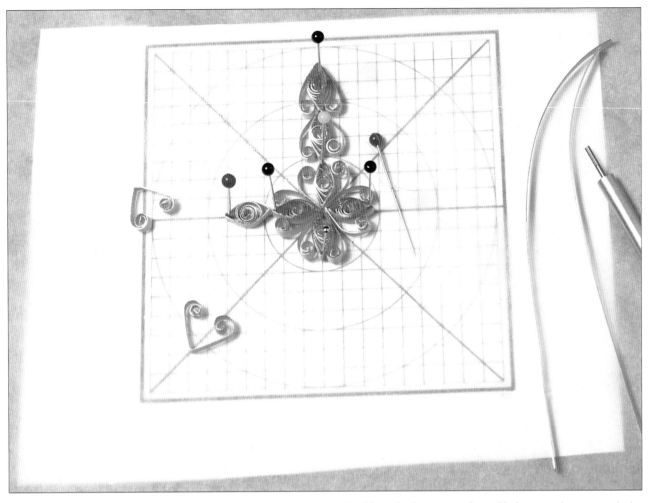

Build up the design on a sheet of baking parchment attached to your work board. A grid is useful for geometric designs.

Quilling boards

A quilling board is a work board on which you can make up your design before attaching it to the surface to be decorated. It is also invaluable for creating free-standing designs, such as Christmas tree decorations.

There are special 'designer boards' on the market. These are made out of cork and on one side have a set of plastic formers which you can use to regulate the size of each coil. These formers are also used for off-centre quilling (see page 167).

You can make your own designer board by sticking rings of different sizes to a backboard. One of my students has a very handy husband who made her a superb designer board out of a sheet of plastic.

A simple board can be made from a square of cork. Cover it with a piece of baking parchment securing it to the cork with drawing pins. If your design is

complicated, then you can place a copy of your pattern under the parchment to use as a guide when sticking. The parchment will also prevent any over-zealously glued coils from sticking to the board. Use pins to hold the glued coils in position while the glue is drying. Alternatively, some students use polystyrene tiles covered with baking parchment. In other words, use whatever comes to hand: as long as you can stick pins in the board, you can use it.

Card/background surfaces

Unless your design is to be three-dimensional, you will need some form of background surface on which to place it. Blank cards can be obtained from several companies who specialize in supplying cards and envelopes – look for advertisements in craft magazines. You can use aperture cards if you wish: I fix a coloured sheet of paper in the aperture area (using double-sided sticky tape) which will tone with my project.

Small cardboard gift boxes can be bought at some stationers. These are lovely if you want to give someone a small present in a very special box – and the box will probably be remembered much more than the present!

You can also decorate place cards for special dinner parties – you can buy these from a card specialist or make your own from some thin card. You can make and then decorate your own Christmas crackers and napkin rings; you can also quill on an egg or anything else that takes your fancy. Quilling does not have to be just on cards – use your imagination. Experienced quillers will often see some object or other and say to themselves, 'Can I quill on that?' The answer is usually 'Yes, I can!'

Other equipment

You will need a tiny pair of sharp scissors for cutting the fringed flowers.

A pair of sharp-pointed tweezers is essential for placing small glued pieces on to your design.

You can make yourself a quilling ruler for one-eighth, one-quarter, one-third, one-half, two-thirds, and three-quarters of a strip of quilling paper. This saves time and frustration when it comes to measuring such things as one-third of a strip. Cut a thin piece of wood to the length of a full strip of quilling paper and then mark the other measurements on it.

Using grids

Geometric grids like those shown on the right are invaluable when you want to make sure that components of a design are straight and square to each other, for instance, when making a cross. Make a photocopy of the grids shown here. Place the grid underneath the baking parchment and you cannot fail to get a good result.

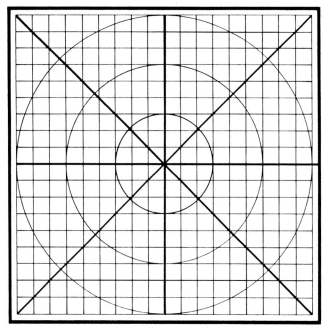

45° grid for use with four- and eight-point star designs.

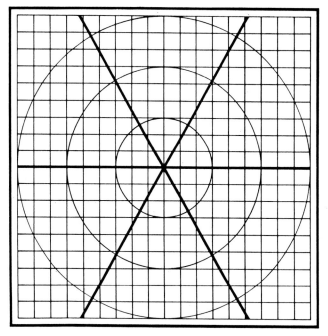

60° grid for use with six-point star designs.

Starting to quill

The best way to learn how to roll your strips of paper is to make a sampler. To do this, firstly make all the shapes, then stick them on to a piece of thin card and write the name of the shape under each piece. A sampler will save you from having to flick backwards and forwards through the book when you are making pieces for a pattern – if you have it in front of you then you will know instantly which shape is required.

I suggest that you use one-quarter-strip lengths of 3mm (1/8in) wide paper for your sampler. Measure the lengths against your quilling ruler and then tear them off. If you use scissors to cut the paper, then you will create a sharp end that will show when you glue the coil closed (a ragged, torn end will hardly show at all). Please note that for clarity the shapes on the sampler shown opposite were made using two-thirds-strips of 10mm (3/8in) wide paper.

To glue your shape to the sampler, simply turn it over on to a board covered with baking parchment, roll a cocktail stick in glue and smear a little on to the back of the shape. It will not need much glue to stick it down, just enough to hold it to the card.

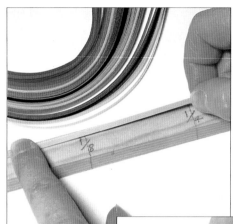

Use a quilling ruler to measure equal lengths of paper.

Tearing the paper to length gives a ragged edge which will become invisible when glued down.

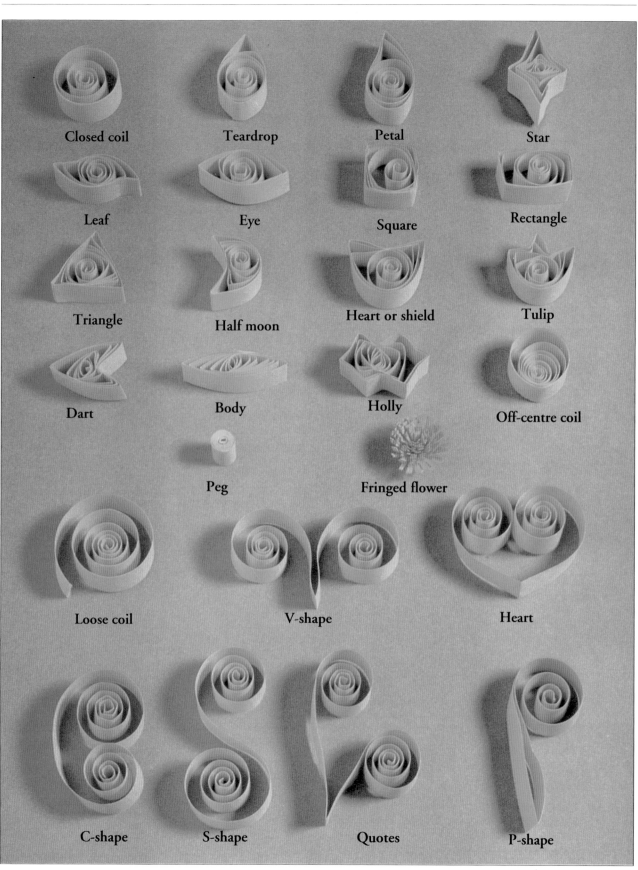

Closed coil

Teardrop

Petal

Star

Leaf

Eye

Square

Rectangle

Triangle

Half moon

Heart or shield

Tulip

Dart

Body

Holly

Off-centre coil

Peg

Fringed flower

Loose coil

V-shape

Heart

C-shape

S-shape

Quotes

P-shape

Rolling a closed coil

Closed coils are used to make most of the mosaic shapes used in quilling designs. The size of the coil will depend upon the length of the quilling paper and the size of the tool used.

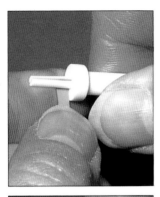

1. Put the end of the quilling paper into the slit in the tool head, making sure that it is resting on the collar of the tool. It should not protrude through the other side of the slit in the head.

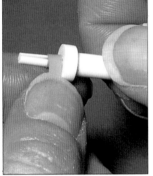

2. Gently roll the tool guiding the paper on to it by letting it run through the thumb and index finger of your other hand. Do not use too much tension or you will screw the head off your quilling tool!

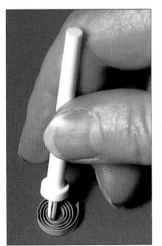

3. When you have finished rolling your piece, turn the tool upside-down and let the coil of paper drop off the tool. You will see it relax just like a watch-spring.

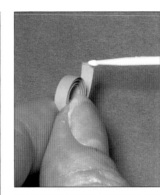

4. Now use a wooden cocktail stick to apply a little glue to the open end. Do not rewind the coil in your hands; you are simply closing it.

5. Use a clean cocktail stick and gently rub the join to make a smooth finish.

To make a good coil, the paper must be evenly rolled. At first, some of you will be loose quillers, some will be too tight, and some of you will make pyramids, like the one shown here, because you have an uneven tension. However, do not worry, practice makes perfect.

Pinching the mosaic shapes

Make a number of same-sized closed coils and then pinch them as described on the following pages to make a variety of mosaic shapes.

1. Teardrop Hold a closed coil in your right hand and pinch the left-hand side to make a teardrop shape. Use this shape for some flower petals.

2. Petal This is a variation of the teardrop shape, so pinch the coil as for a teardrop and then turn the pinched end down slightly to curve the top.

5. Star Pinch the coil as for the eye shape and then (still holding the ends) push the thumbs and fingers towards each other so that they meet. This makes lovely holly with one-quarter- or one-eighth-strip lengths of paper.

6. Square Hold the coil vertically between your index finger and thumb of one hand, and with your other index finger and thumb, gently close the fingers to form a square shape. . .

. . . When the basic shape has been formed, pinch all four corners to sharpen the shape.

3. Eye Take the coil between the thumb and index finger of both hands, then pinch both sides of the coil to make an eye shape.

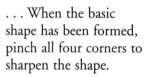

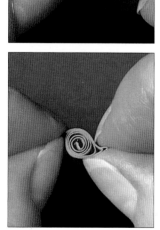

4. Leaf Pinch the coil as for the eye shape and then (still holding the ends) move your left hand upwards and the right hand downwards to complete the shape.

7. Rectangle This is made in a similar way to the square – your right-hand thumb and finger make the longer sides and your other thumb or finger make the short sides. Pinch the corners sharp after forming.

8. Triangle Place a coil between the tips of your index fingers and thumbs. Keeping the tips of your fingers together bring up both thumbs to form the shape. Pinch each corner to sharpen up the shape.

9. Half moon Hold the coil in one hand then, using the handle end of a quilling tool as a former, push the coil against the tool to form the shape. Pinch the two corners.

10. Heart or shield Hold the coil in the left hand, push the edge of the coil inwards with the index finger of the other hand and pinch the edges round the finger. Carefully squeeze the corners to complete the shape.

11. Tulip Make a teardrop shape and, still holding the pinched end, move it inwards to form the shape.

12. Dart Pinch as for a teardrop then, holding the pinched end in the left hand, push the right index finger into the coil until the rounded ends come up over your finger. Pinch the corners to make a sharp arrow-head shape.

13. Body Take a coil and squash it, making a sharp point at each end. This is used for simple butterfly and dragon-fly bodies.

14. Holly This shape is best made with paper strips that are over one-quarter of a length. Using a pair of tweezers, pinch the top and bottom of the coil together. Now, pinch one of the sides between your index finger and thumb and push the pinched end towards the tweezers. Still holding the tweezers closed, change hands and repeat at the other end.

Rolling off-centre coils

Off-centre coils are made on a designer board (see page 160). They are used to make mosaic shapes slightly different in appearance to those made from simple closed coils.

1. Roll your coil and glue it closed. Place it into the right size former on the designer board. If you are using gilded or pearl-edged paper you must place the coil into the former with the gilded or pearlised edge down.

2. Use a pearl-headed pin to pull the centre of the coil towards the edge of the former, then push the pin into the board.

3. Using a cocktail stick, rub glue into the area between the pin and the edge of the former, and leave it to dry. Remember that the side you have glued is the *back* of the coil.

4. When the glue is dry, gently twist the pin, and remove it and the off-centre coil from the board.

5. The basic coil can be used to make the mosaic shapes on the sampler. When pinching shapes ensure that the off-centre is at the place in which you want the colour intensified. For instance, in a teardrop the centre will be at the rounded end of the shape.

Rolling a peg

Pegs are tightly rolled lengths of paper that can be used for the centres of flowers and to provide small dense areas of colour.

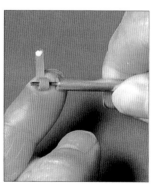

1. Put a little glue on one end of the paper and roll it up on the tool from the non-glued end to form a tightly closed peg. Hold the paper until the glue dries.

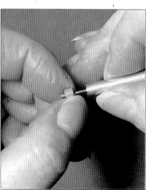

2. Gently ease the peg off the tool using your finger and thumb.

Making fringed flowers

Fringed flowers are made in much the same way as pegs but you use a fringed length of 7mm (⁹/₃₂in) or 10mm (³/₈in) quilling paper.

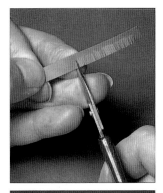

1. Use a one-quarter length of paper and with tiny sharp scissors make a cut three-quarters of the way across its width. Continue cutting in this way along the whole length to make a fringe of paper.

2. Glue and roll the strip as for a peg (see page 167) making sure that the uncut edge is against the collar of the tool. Using your fingers, spread the fringing to produce a pompon-type flower.

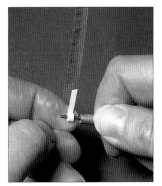

3. To make a flower with a centre, glue a strip of 3mm (¹/₈in) paper to the end of the fringed piece and roll from the 3mm (¹/₈in) end.

Two completed fringed flowers – one without a centre and one with a centre in a contrasting colour.

Filigree shapes

These shapes look like wrought-iron work. They are rolled without glue. Use one-eighth-strip lengths of paper for your sampler. Many variations are possible.

1. **Loose coil** Roll a coil and let it drop off the tool but do not glue the end. This is often used when you are filling in shapes in more advanced quilling.

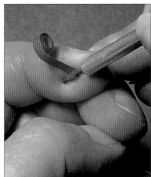

2. **S-shape** Roll one end of a strip to about the mid-point and let it drop off the tool. Turn the strip and roll the other end in the same way. When using gilded-edged paper you may want some reverse-S-shape pieces.

3. **C-shape** This is a variation of the S-shape but you roll both ends of the paper towards the middle.

4. **Heart** Fold the strip in half, pinch the fold and then roll each end of the strip inwards towards the fold line.

5. V-shape Fold the strip in half, pinch the fold and then roll each end of the paper outwards towards the fold line. This shape makes wonderful antennae for butterflies.

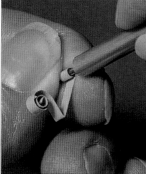

6. Quotes Fold the paper in half, pinch the fold and then roll one end outwards towards the fold and the other inwards (same direction) towards the fold.

7. P-shape Fold the paper in half and pinch the fold. Place both end pieces into the quilling tool and roll downwards towards the fold. One piece of paper will bow slightly and this is correct.

Making up flowers

Make up complete flowers on your quilling board before sticking them on to your card. Try different arrangements then, when you are satisfied, glue them down and add leaves and other small pieces.

To make up a complete flower, place one shape on your board and put a pin through its centre to stop it from slipping. Take a second shape and spread a little glue along the outside at the point where it will touch the first shape. Place it next to the first shape and lightly press the two together. Again, place a pin through the second shape to hold it in position. Following your pattern, or making up the design as you go along, stick and pin the rest of the shapes until the flower is completed. Once the glue has dried, remove the pins and lift the flower from the board.

Easy first projects

It is a good idea to start by decorating a small flat surface, so in this section I have included a variety of simple greetings card designs for you to try.

Dog roses card

Materials

Blank greetings card

3mm ($1/8$in) quilling paper

5mm ($3/16$in) quilling paper for fringed flowers

Shapes

You will need to quill the following:

PETALS – ten one-third-strip heart shapes

CENTRES – two fringed flowers made from one-third-strips attached to 3cm ($1 1/4$in) lengths of 5mm ($3/16$in) fringed paper

LEAVES – twenty-four one-eighth-strip teardrops

STEMS AND STALKS – shorts strips glued on their sides

Making up the design

Glue sets of three and five teardrop shapes together on the board to form the leaves. Cut a small slot at one end of a short strip (a stalk) and push each side of the slot outwards to make a 'platform'. Apply glue to the platform, position it across the bottom of the leaf assembly and then smooth each side of the platform into place. You can use this method to attach stalks to individual leaf shapes on other designs.

Make up each flower on the board. Glue the left-hand flower on to the card, then glue the second one so that one of its petals comes up and over the first flower. This gives a three-dimensional effect to your work. Quilling does *not* have to be flat!

Glue the leaf clusters and stems into place on the card. You will notice that the long stem from the left-hand flower has been looped at the bottom and the excess looped paper glued to one side – if you want to do the same on your card you must pinch the loops into the paper before you glue it on to the card.

Make two flaps in the end of a stalk and stick this 'platform' around the end of the leaf cluster.

A selection of greetings cards. From the left: Exotic lotus card (page 173), dog roses card (opposite) and best wishes card (page 172).

Best wishes card

Materials
Blank greetings card

3mm (¹/₈in) quilling paper

Shapes
You will need to quill the following:

PETALS – ten one-quarter-strip closed coils

    – thirteen one-quarter-strip teardrops

CENTRES – five one-eighth-strip closed coils

LEAVES – eight one-quarter-strip leaf shapes

BUTTERFLY BODY – one one-eighth-strip body shape

WINGS – four one-quarter-strip teardrops

ANTENNAE – a short strip rolled into a V-shape

Detail of flowers for best wishes card

BEST WISHES

Making up the design

THE GREETING I am a great believer in mixing and matching crafts and in this case the greeting has been done using a brass stencil and the technique known as embossing on paper. You can omit the greeting if you like, or perhaps your handwriting is better than mine and you can write it on. The other alternative is to trace the greeting, turn the paper over and scribble on the back and then place it on your card and trace over it again – this way you can see the outline of the greeting and perhaps use a gold pen to write over it. Whichever way you choose, the greeting has to be put on before the quilling.

THE QUILLED DESIGN Make up each flower completely on the quilling board, then the butterfly without its antennae. Arrange these on to your card and then stick them down by rolling the cocktail stick into the glue and then over the back of each piece. Glue down the antennae and glue the leaves into place.

Exotic lotus card

Materials

Blank greetings card

3mm (¹/₈in) quilling paper

A needle at least 3.75cm (1¹/₂in) in length. A well-polished No.14 knitting needle will do, although an American needle tool is better

Shapes

For this card, the petals are made from modified leaf shapes. Use three shades of the same colour to achieve a better effect. You will need to quill the following:

FLOWER CENTRE – one one-half-strip eye shape (pale shade of paper)

PETALS – four full-strip leaf shapes (dark shade)

– four full-strip leaf shapes (medium shade)

– two one-half-strip leaf shapes (pale shade)

– two one-quarter-strip leaf shapes (pale shade)

LEAVES – three one-half-strip leaf shapes

– one one-quarter-strip leaf shape

STEM – one one-quarter-strip spiral

Making up the design

To make a spiral you must use a needle tool. Wrap the end of the paper around the needle and then come slightly off-centre. With the thumb and finger of the right hand guiding the paper, turn the needle with the left hand, thus creating a spiral rope. You will find that at some stage the spiral comes off the top of the needle. Do not worry; this is quite normal.

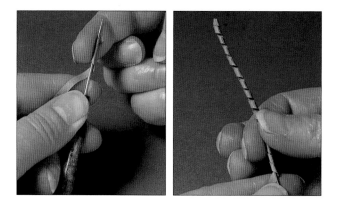

Make up the flower, with its stalk attached at the flower head, on the quilling board. Apply glue to the flower head, and also apply small dots of glue along the spiral. Holding the end of the spiral away from the card, secure the head in place and then bend the spiral to make the desired stalk shape. Hold it in place until dry, then attach the leaves.

Projects for special occasions

There are many occasions which call for a card handmade with love – the birth of a baby, a christening, weddings, First Communions, wedding anniversaries and bereavements. Here are some ideas for you.

New baby/christening card

Materials

Blank greetings card

1.5mm (¹/₁₆in) or 3mm (¹/₈in) quilling paper

Three embroidery beads or pearls and all-purpose glue (optional)

Shapes

I used 1.5mm (¹/₁₆in) paper for this design, but you can of course use 3mm (¹/₈in) paper. I also used small pearls for the three flower centres, but you could use pegs instead. The top and bottom layers of the flowers use the same shapes but, for greater impact, I used two shades of the same colour for each flower. You will need to quill the following:

FLOWERS – twenty-four one-sixth-strip eye shapes

– twelve one-sixth-strip teardrop shapes

FLOWER CENTRES – three beads or pearls, or three one-eighth-strip pegs

PEG FLOWERS – ten one-eighth-strip pegs
          – eight one-sixteenth-strip pegs

STEMS – strips of paper glued on their sides

TENDRILS – ten one-eighth-strip loose coils
          – four one-eighth-strip V-shapes

Making up the design

THE CARD This card is shaped like a baby's bib and was cut from a larger card. Trace the bib outline, scribble over the back of the outline, then place the top of the bib on to the fold line of the card and draw around the outer and neck edges. Cut it out.

THE QUILLED DESIGN Make up the flowers on the quilling board and then position each one on the card and glue it down. From strips of paper, make the stems extending from each flower towards the middle (use the pattern as a guide). Glue the V-shapes into place and then glue the loose-coil tendrils into place. Arrange the peg flowers along the top two stems on each side of the central flower and glue into place. Finally, if you are using them, glue the pearls to the centres of the large flowers.

From the left: Christening/wedding bonbonnière and new baby/christening card (opposite).

First Communion or condolence card

Materials

Dark-coloured blank greetings card

3mm ($\frac{1}{8}$in) quilling paper

For a First Communion card use a white or silver-edged white paper, but for a condolence card a pale lilac or pearl-edged lilac paper would be more suitable.

Shapes

You will need to quill the following:

CROSS	– nine one-quarter-strip eye shapes
	– thirteen one-eighth-strip filigree heart shapes
	– eight one-eighth-strip pegs
	– one one-quarter-strip closed coil
INITIALS	– six one-eighth-strip teardrops
	– three one-eighth-strip eye shapes
	– one one-eighth-strip peg

Making up the design

Put a 45° grid under the baking parchment on your quilling board and use the cross lines as a guide when assembling the cross.

Glue four of the eye shapes inside four of the heart shapes at the fold line. Put a dab of glue on either side of each eye shape, about three-quarters of the way up, and attach each side of the heart to these points.

Now, glue these four pieces together to form the centre of the cross, making sure that each eye shape is on the lines of the grid to keep it square. Glue the closed coil above the centre point of the cross.

Next, glue the other five eye shapes to five heart shapes at the fold line. Put a little dab of glue on either side of the other end of the eye shape, bring up each side of the heart and attach them to these points.

Assemble one of these pieces to each arm of the central cross and place the final one below one of these pieces to form the bottom portion of the cross.

Glue the other four heart shapes to the end of each arm of the cross. Glue a peg inside each heart-shaped end and also at the joint of each heart that makes up the centre of the cross.

Finally, transfer the design on to your card. If you want to personalise the card you can make up and glue on the initials of the recipient (in this case I used the initials IHS).

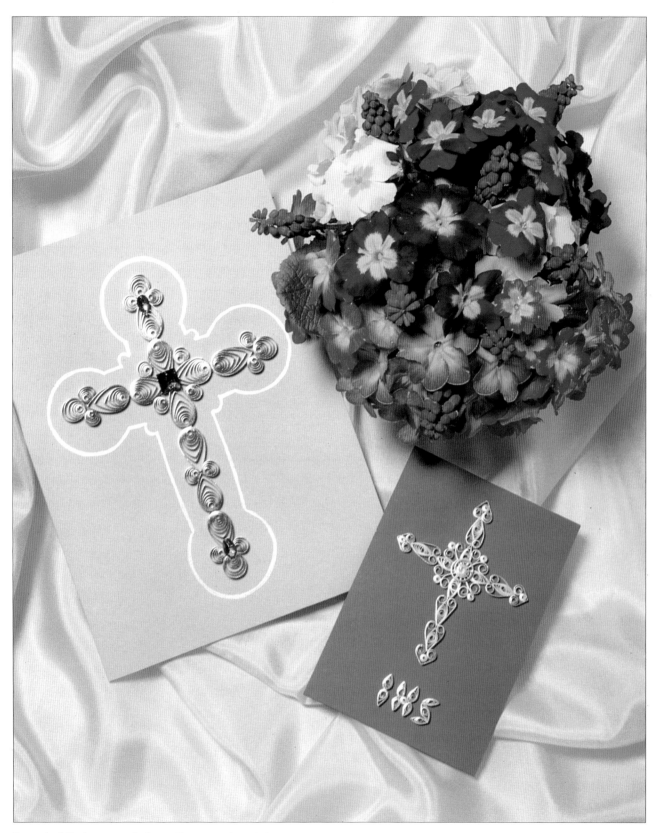

From the left: A cross made from off-centre coils and decorated with embroidery stones, and the First Communion card (opposite).

A wedding horseshoe

Give a bride a special reminder of her wedding day!

Materials

Piece of shiny silver card

Length of white 12mm (½in) wide ribbon

Two small white sticky labels

3mm (⅛in) quilling paper

7 or 10mm (⁹⁄₃₂in or ⅜in) quilling paper for the ribbon roses

All-purpose glue

Shapes

You will need to quill the following:

HORSESHOE – approximately fifty-two one-eighth-strip C-shapes (white or silver-edged white)

LEAVES – twenty one-eighth-strip teardrop shapes

STEMS – short strips glued on their sides

RIBBON ROSES – two 29cm (11½in) strips
– one 15cm (6in) strip
– one 10cm (4in) strip
– one 5cm (2in) strip

See overleaf for details of making ribbon roses.

Making up the design

THE HORSESHOE Using a soft pencil, trace the horseshoe shape on to a piece of paper and place it pencil-side down on to the white back of the silver card. Draw over the pencil line and remove the tracing paper. Carefully cut out the horseshoe.

Place one end of the ribbon behind one side of the horseshoe and fix into place with a sticky label (this covers the raw edges as well). Decide how long you want the ribbon to be, then cut it to size and fix the other end into place.

Remember to write on the back of the horseshoe who it is from *before* you start quilling.

THE QUILLED DESIGN Use a long-headed beginner's tool with a collar to make the ribbon roses. Roll the paper around a couple of times to secure it, then fold the paper down at right angles and continue rolling carefully until the paper straightens out again. Turn down again and continue until the paper straightens out – repeat this process until you come to the end of the paper. Then, turn the end down and carefully

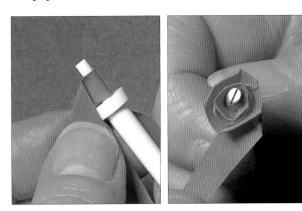

After a couple of turns, fold the paper down at right angles. . .   *. . . and continue turning and folding to build up the shape.*

remove the rose with your forefinger on the rose centre and your thumb supporting the bottom. Let it uncoil a little, but be careful or it will come completely undone! Apply glue to the bottom of the rose, making sure that the centre also catches the glue, and then press down the end of the paper over the bottom of the rose and hold in position until dry. I suggest that you practise on a spare piece of paper to get the technique right before making the actual roses for the horseshoe.

Make up the sets of leaves and stems using the technique explained on page 170, sticking the platform to one teardrop and then sticking the other teardrops on either side of the stem. Leave to dry.

You will need to use all-purpose or tacky glue to stick the pieces on to the horseshoe. Position the ribbon roses on the horseshoe shape and glue into place. Shorten the stems of the rose leaves as required and glue them into place.

Finally, glue the C-shapes around the edges (straight sides to the middle). If you have spaces that will not take a full C-shape, make loose coils from about one-sixteenth of a strip of paper and use these instead.

Flowers in a shoe – a special wedding memento

You can make this as a picture and add the bride's and groom's names and date of the wedding, or you could make it into a very special card. The choice is yours.

Materials
Piece of card

3mm ($\frac{1}{8}$in) quilling paper

Coloured inks, paints, or felt-tipped pens

Shapes
This design includes three different types of flower, each of which needs to be made up before being attached to the card.

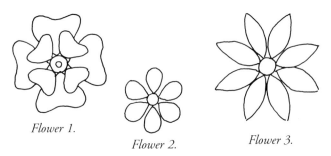

Flower 1.   *Flower 2.*   *Flower 3.*

FLOWER 1 (make three of these flowers)

BOTTOM LAYER – four one-third-strip heart shapes

TOP LAYER – four one-eighth-strip heart shapes

CENTRE – one one-quarter-strip bell shape

This shape is based on the principle of a peg, but after two or three turns of the tool let the paper go off-centre and keep rolling. Glue closed as for a peg and then carefully remove the conical shape from the tool. Glue the inside of the cone to stop it collapsing.

To make this flower, glue the four bottom petals around the base of the bell shape and then stick the four small petals on the top of them.

FLOWER 2 (make three of these flowers)

CENTRE – one one-eighth-strip peg

PETALS – six one-eighth-strip teardrop shapes

To make this flower, glue the petals around the peg.

FLOWER 3 (complete)

PETALS – eight one-quarter-strip eye shapes

CENTRE – one one-quarter-strip bell shape

FLOWER 3 (half)

PETALS – four one-quarter-strip eye shapes
– two one-eighth-strip eye shapes

CENTRE – one one-quarter-strip bell shape

To make up the complete flower, glue eight petals around the bell shape. The half flower is made from four petals glued to the bell shape with the two smaller petals at each side.

LEAVES

MODIFIED LEAF SHAPES – fourteen one-eighth-strip closed coils made into semicircular shapes (seven in light green and seven in dark green)

Glue the light-green semicircles to the dark-green ones along the straight edges and when dry modify each piece into a leaf shape.

SHOE

S-SHAPES – about forty one-eighth-strip S-shapes

Making up the design

First, make a tracing of the shoe outline and transfer it to your card. The inner heel can be painted in with ink, paint, or felt-tipped pen, using a colour similar to that of the shoe. In this example, I used a silver marker pen to complement the silver-edged white quilling paper used for the S-shapes. The bow on the back of the shoe is made from two loops of paper with two short strips for the 'tails'.

Arrange the made-up flowers on the shoe as shown on the pattern. Remember to let some flowers overlap others to give dimension to the finished piece.

Finally, fill the outline with the S-shapes. If you want to give the shoe a definite outline glue a strip of paper around the outer contour of the shoe, gluing it to the outer edges of the S-shapes.

Projects for festivals

It is nice to send family and friends handmade cards at Christmas and Easter, but you can also make three-dimensional decorations for your Christmas tree. In this section, I have included two tree decorations for you to try, as well as a design for an Easter card.

A Christmas tree

Materials

3, 5, or 7mm ($^1/_8$, $^3/_{16}$, or $^9/_{32}$in) quilling paper

Length of thread for a hanger

7cm ($2^3/_4$in) length of square balsa wood, obtainable from any good model shop

The width of paper you use will determine the width of the balsa wood, so if you use 5mm ($^3/_{16}$in) paper then you need 5mm ($^3/_{16}$in) square balsa wood.

Shapes

Referring to the pattern, make up four sets of closed coils using the various lengths of paper as indicated, and then modify each one to the shape shown on the pattern (the bottom section is the tree tub).

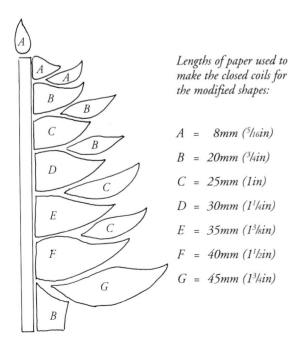

Lengths of paper used to make the closed coils for the modified shapes:

A = 8mm ($^5/_{16}$in)

B = 20mm ($^3/_4$in)

C = 25mm (1in)

D = 30mm ($1^1/_4$in)

E = 35mm ($1^3/_8$in)

F = 40mm ($1^1/_2$in)

G = 45mm ($1^3/_4$in)

Making up the design

Trace the pattern for the branches and tub on to baking parchment as a guide for assembling the tree. Start at the bottom and build up a section of the tree by gluing the leaf pieces together, making sure that you have a good straight edge down the left-hand side. Make up four sections.

Next, glue two quilled sections to the balsa-wood trunk, one on either side, then glue the third section to the top edge of the trunk (you may have to hold it in place until the glue dries if it starts slipping). Wait until these sections are really dry and then glue on the fourth section – again you must hold it in place until the glue has dried. Finally, glue the teardrop finial to the top of the trunk. Now, if you want to, you can decorate the tree with sequins and glitter.

When everything is dry, pass a thread through the top of the teardrop shape to make a hanger.

Candle in a ring

Materials

3mm ($^1/_8$in) quilling paper

Two lengths of silver thread

Circular object, such as a jar lid

Shapes

You will need to quill the following:

RING – thirty-six one-eighth-strip closed coils (half in red and half in green)

CANDLE – four one-eighth-strip closed coils (in white)

CANDLE FLAME – one petal shape made from a one-sixteenth-strip of orange paper glued to a one-eighth-strip of yellow paper

HOLLY – six one-eighth-strip star shapes (in green)

BERRIES – seven one-eighth-strip pegs (in red)

HANGERS – one one-eighth-strip open peg wound around the handle of the quilling tool (outer)
– one one-eighth-strip peg (inner)

Making up the design

Fasten a clean piece of baking parchment to your quilling board and draw around a circular object, e.g. a jar lid. My circle was 7cm (2¾in) in diameter.

Glue the closed coils together, using the circle on the baking parchment as a guide and pins to keep them in position. Alternate the colours. Stick the top hanger to the outside of the circle and the peg hanger directly underneath. Then glue the four white coils together, using a straight line as a guide, and attach the flame.

Glue two holly leaves and a berry to each side of the candle (between the third and fourth coils) and three berries in a pyramid shape to the bottom of the candle. Glue a holly leaf and berry over the bottom coil of the candle and repeat this on the other side.

Attach the candle to the inner top hanger by passing a silver thread through the centre of the peg and the top of the candle flame. Tie a knot in the thread when the candle is hanging in the middle of the circle. Pass another piece of silver thread through the top hanger and make a loop to hang on the tree.

Do try experimenting. Here, I have used quilling to decorate a candle and a paper bauble.

Easter card

Materials

Three-fold oval greetings card with an aperture

3mm (¹/₈in) quilling paper

Dark-green paper

Shapes

FILIGREE CROSS – follow the instructions given for the First Communion or condolence card on page 176 to make the filigree cross, omitting the closed coil on top of the central cross. I used yellow pearl-edged paper for my cross.

Enlarged view of miniature daffodils.

DAFFODILS – make nine miniature daffodils. Cut three 2cm (³/₄in) long strips of 3mm (¹/₈in) white paper and glue them together as shown. With a pair of quilling scissors, cut the ends of the paper strips to points and gently curl the paper upwards.

Using a 3cm (1¹/₄in) strip of orange paper, wrap this around the handle of the quilling tool and glue it closed as an open peg. Glue this to the centre of the crossed strips of white paper.

Making up the design

First, stick the dark-green paper inside the aperture of the card to give a background to the design. Next, glue the filigree cross into place on the card.

Finally, glue one daffodil to the centre of the cross and position the others as shown.

This is a good example of the way in which you can adapt a quilling pattern to suit any occasion.

Advanced projects

Parasol with flowers

Here is a card for any occasion – you can use the parasol by itself or add flowers to your own taste.

Most of the parasol is made from *huskings*. This is an eighteenth-century technique in which the paper is wound around pins to give the shape required. By altering the position of the pins you can make different sizes and shapes of huskings. In the eighteenth century ladies used these to produce even shapes to decorate the borders of boxes and pictures.

Materials

Blank greetings card

3mm ($\frac{1}{8}$in) quilling paper

1.5mm ($\frac{1}{16}$in) quilling paper

Shapes

You will need to quill the following:

FLOWERS You can make any flowers you like, but if you want to make them the same as mine, then choose 3mm ($\frac{1}{8}$in) paper in a colour similar to your background and make:

> – thirty-five one-eighth-strip teardrops
> – seven one-eighth-strip pegs

LEAVES   – six one-eighth-strip leaf shapes

PARASOL – five four-pin huskings (see opposite)

> – three one-third-strip pegs, one made from 3mm ($\frac{1}{8}$in) and two from 1.5mm ($\frac{1}{16}$in) paper (the same colour as the huskings)
> – ten one-eighth-strip C-shapes
> – five one-eighth-strip S-shapes
> – one one-quarter-strip triangle
> – one one-quarter-strip closed coil
> – 45mm ($1\frac{3}{4}$in) strip for the handle
> – 15mm ($\frac{5}{8}$in) strip for the ferrule
> – short strips for the bow

Making up the design

First, make up all the individual huskings and flowers on the board and put them to one side.

Now, apply glue to the long side of each husking and stick them together – I used two pins to keep the

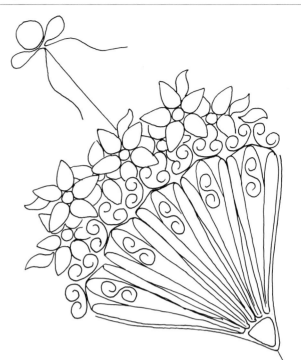

bottom edge of the huskings close together. Glue the triangle to the bottom of the huskings. Now, to hold the parasol together, glue a strip of gilded paper from the top of one long edge, around the triangle and up to the top of the other side.

Next glue the S-shapes into the huskings and the C-shapes to the top edge of the parasol, positioning them as shown in the diagram.

Lay the parasol, together with the handle, its closed-coil end, and the ferrule on the card and adjust them until you get the best angle.

Glue the 3mm ($\frac{1}{8}$in) peg under the parasol, beneath the join of the middle two C-shapes, and the two 1.5mm ($\frac{1}{16}$in) pegs similarly, halfway between each side and the middle peg. These will raise your parasol from the card in a realistic manner.

Now apply glue to the three pegs, to the two long outer edges of the huskings and also to the triangle, and stick them to your card. Glue the handle strip into place on its side and add the closed coil. Glue the ferrule on its side.

Make two loops from 3mm ($\frac{1}{8}$in) paper and glue one on each side of handle under the knob – shape two more strips of paper for the ribbon ends and glue them into place under the loops.

Finally, arrange the flowers – I have four flowers stuck directly to the card and three flowers stuck on top of those. Glue the leaves into place.

How to make huskings

1. Copy the pin placings on to the baking parchment on your designer board (number them until you get used to making huskings).

3. Now wind the paper around pin 3, back to pin 1, up around pin 4 and back down to pin 1 again.

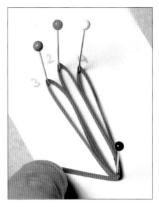

2. Push a pin into each placing and then, starting at pin 1, wind the paper up around pin 2 and back to pin 1.

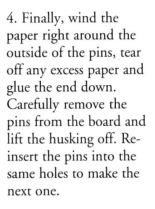

4. Finally, wind the paper right around the outside of the pins, tear off any excess paper and glue the end down. Carefully remove the pins from the board and lift the husking off. Re-insert the pins into the same holes to make the next one.

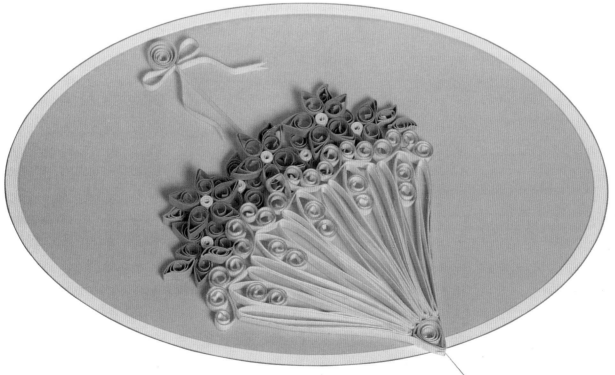

A bouquet of flowers

Materials

Blank greetings card

55mm (2¼in) posy frill or ruff, obtainable from quilling specialist suppliers

3mm (⅛in) quilling paper

7mm (⁹⁄₃₂in) quilling paper

10mm (³⁄₈in) quilling paper

Shapes

You will need to quill the following:

POSY RUFF
   – one 3mm (⅛in) two-thirds-strip loose coil
   – one 7mm (⁹⁄₃₂in) one-quarter-strip peg
   – strips of 3mm (⅛in) paper for double bow

You can fill the posy ruff with any flowers you like, but if you want to make them like mine then you will need the following:

FRINGED FLOWERS
   – four, each one made from a one-quarter-strip of 10mm (³⁄₈in) paper with a centre made from a one-eighth-strip of 3mm (⅛in) paper

   – one made from a one-eighth-strip of 7mm (⁹⁄₃₂in) paper with a centre made from a one-sixteenth-strip of 3mm (⅛in) paper

   – three, each made from a one-eighth-strip of 7mm (⁹⁄₃₂in) paper but with *no* centres

The following are all made from 3mm (⅛in) paper:

PEG BUDS
   – seven one-eighth-strip pegs
   – eight one-twelfth-strip pegs
   – twelve one-sixteenth-strip pegs

LEAVES
   – four one-quarter-strip leaf shapes

Tendrils
   – two one-eighth-strip V-shapes

STEMS
   – short strips glued on their sides

Making up the design

Make up three spire-like flowers. First, glue a stem to one of the smallest peg flowers using the method for assembling leaves (see page 172). Now, apply glue down the two sides of the stem and arrange a further two of the smallest pegs, two of the mid-sized pegs and two of the large ones down the stem. Make the other pegs into oval buds, by pressing between your finger and thumb, the glue them to other stems.

Put some glue into the shaped centre of the posy ruff, drop the loose coil into it and arrange it with your finger! This gives a better surface for the flowers.

Now glue the 7mm (⁹⁄₃₂in) wide peg on to the back of the posy ruff as a support. Glue the posy ruff to the card by applying glue to the peg and to the edge of the ruff opposite the peg. This will cant the posy ruff at an angle. Add a double bow and ribbon ends to the glued-down edge of the posy ruff.

Finally, arrange the flowers and foliage in the posy ruff as you wish and glue into place.

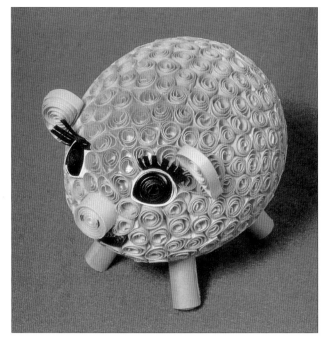

Three-dimensional quilling can be particularly creative and humerous. This little pig started out life as a blown hen's egg.

Some examples of miniature quilling. The planters (above) were made for a doll's house. The basket of flowers (right), at a slightly larger scale, was made to decorate a glass cabinet.

A blown goose egg decorated with quilling. The stand is also made from quilling paper.

And finally...

I do hope that you have enjoyed this taste of quilling and the other papercrafts in this book, and that you feel inspired to create your own designs.

Inspiration for designs can come from all sorts of places, such as wallpaper, embroidery patterns, botanical paintings and books. Make notes about the materials you use, so that you can find them again when you want to make a similar design. Keep all leftovers in a box so that you can use them at a later date. If you want to make a card in a hurry you may be glad of your 'bits and pieces' box.

A great many people look at my papercraft work and say that they did not realise how intricate and beautiful finished pieces can be. Once you have learnt the basic techniques, the only boundaries are those of your imagination. You *can* become an expert – it may take a little time and patience, but then, you cannot create a work of art in a few minutes. Just remember that the more you do the better you will become.

Index

First published in Great Britain 2000

Search Press Limited
Wellwood, North Farm Road, Tunbridge Wells, Kent TN2 3DR

Reprinted 2002, 2003

Based on the following books by Janet Wilson, published by
Search Press, Tunbridge Wells:

Parchment Craft, copyright © Search Press Ltd. 1995
The Craft of Quilling, copyright © Search Press Ltd. 1996
The Art of Parchment Craft, copyright © Janet Wilson 1997
The Art of Decorative Paper Pricking, copyright © Janet Wilson 1998
The Art of Stencil Embossing, copyright © Janet Wilson 2000

Photographs by Search Press Studios
Photographs and design copyright © Search Press Ltd. 2000

ISBN 0 85532 928 9

Readers are permitted to reproduce any of the patterns in this
book for their personal use, or for the purposes of selling for
charity, free of charge and without the prior permission of the
Publishers. Any use of the patterns for commercial purposes is
not permitted without the prior permission of the Publishers.

The Publishers and author can accept no responsibility for any
consequences arising from the information, advice or
instructions given in this publication.

Suppliers
If you have difficulty in obtaining any of the materials and
equipment mentioned in this book, then please visit the
Search Press website for details of suppliers: www.searchpress.com

Alternatively, you can write to the Publishers at the address
above, for a current list of stockists, which includes firms who
operate a mail-order service.

Publishers' note
All the step-by-step photographs in this book feature the
author, Janet Wilson, demonstrating traditional papercraft
techniques. No models have been used.

Parchment tool sizes: all parchment tools mentioned in
this book are manufactured to metric measurements.
The following is a list of the tools used together with the
nearest imperial equivalent.

1mm (0.040in)

1.5mm (0.060in)

3mm (0.120in)

4mm (0.160in)

Colour separation by Graphics '91 Pte Ltd, Singapore
Printed in Malaysia by Times Offset (M) Sdn Bhd